MW01702645

MEET THE CHIEF!

A FUN LOOK AT THE U.S. PRESIDENTS

JOEL F. KING

First printing: 2011
First Master Books revised edition: February 2021

Copyright © 2011, 2021 by Joel F. King and Master Books®. All rights reserved. No part of this book may be reproduced, copied, broadcast, stored, or shared in any form whatsoever without written permission from the publisher, except in the case of brief quotations in articles and reviews. For information write:

Master Books®, P.O. Box 726, Green Forest, AR 72638

Master Books® is a division of the New Leaf Publishing Group, Inc.

ISBN: 978-1-68344-273-8
ISBN: 978-1-61458-774-3 (digital)

Library of Congress Number: 2021931788

Cover Design: Diana Bogardus
Interior Design: Terry White

Unless otherwise noted, Scripture quotations are from the King James Version (KVJ).

Please consider requesting that a copy of this volume be purchased by your local library system.

Printed in the United States

Please visit our website for other great titles:
www.masterbooks.com

Dedication: To my parents, Joe and Margaret King, for inspiring my love for history.

Master Books®
A Division of New Leaf Publishing Group
www.masterbooks.com

Joel King is a homeschool dad with a passion for creating educational resources with unique twists. He loves to play games with his three boys and believes that children retain knowledge better when having fun. Joel has a B.S. degree in accounting from the University of Kentucky and works as a state auditor. He lives with his wife and three boys in western Kentucky, where they have homeschooled for 25 years.

Table of Contents

All images are getty.com, or public domain (CC0 1.0), (CC BY 2.0), (CC BY-NC 2.0), (CC BY 2.5), (CC BY-SA2.0), (CC BY 3.0), (CC BY-SA 3.0), (CC BY 4.0), (CC BY-SA 4.0).

Introduction

Since the first presidential inauguration in 1789, the United States has sought strong leadership. But just who can be president and what can they do?

Who can be president?

According to Article II of the U.S. Constitution, the president of the United States must

- ☆ be a natural-born citizen of the United States;
- ☆ be at least 35 years old;
- ☆ have been a permanent resident in the United States for at least 14 years.

What is the president's job?

The U.S. government is composed of three branches.

- ☆ The legislative branch consists of the Senate and the House of Representatives. Together, the Senate and House are called Congress, and their primary task is to write laws.
- ☆ The judicial branch consists of the federal courts and the Supreme Court. Their primary job is to interpret the law.
- ☆ The executive branch is made up of the president, the vice president, and others who help the president. Their primary job is to execute the law.

As head of the executive branch, the president has a lot of power and responsibility. The president

- ☆ can sign or veto legislation;
- ☆ is commander-in-chief and commands the military;
- ☆ takes care that the laws are faithfully executed;
- ☆ appoints ambassadors and federal officers;
- ☆ nominates federal judges;
- ☆ can grant pardons and reprieves.

John F. Kennedy #35
1961-1963
Democrat
Born: May 29, 1917
Died: November 22, 1963

1961
- John F. Kennedy takes office
- The Bay of Pigs fiasco takes place in Cuba
- The Berlin Wall is constructed in Germany
- Alan Shepard becomes the first American to enter space

1962
- The Cuban Missile Crisis unfolds
- The U.S. and Russia escalate nuclear weapons testing

1963
- Martin Luther King Jr. makes his "I Have A Dream" speech
- President Kennedy is assassinated

President Trivia Games
Who Am I? 2001-2009 See page 92
Trivia: Who was the second president of the United States? See page 10

John F. Kennedy was born in 1917 in Massachusetts and graduated from Harvard College with a degree in international affairs in 1941. As tensions were pointing to World War II, he volunteered for the U.S. Army but was rejected due to back problems. However, the U.S. Navy gladly took him aboard.

President John F. Kennedy Meeting of the Executive Committee of the National Security Council

Lieutenant John F. Kennedy being awarded the Navy and Marine Corps Medal for heroism in rescuing members of the crew of the PT-109

John F. Kennedy commanded a PT boat during World War II. He received several medals for his service and obtained the rank of lieutenant. Kennedy became a hero during the war for his service aboard PT-109 (a torpedo patrol boat). After the war ended, he began his political career, which included him being elected to the U.S. House of Representatives in 1946 and the U.S. Senate in 1952. Four years later, he nearly became the Democratic Party's vice-presidential nominee; however, in 1960, he fared much better. He became his party's nominee for the nation's top prize, the presidency.

Kennedy became president by winning the 1960 election. During his term, he confronted the spread of Communism throughout the world. The most memorable moment occurred when the U.S. stopped the Soviet Union from building nuclear missile sites in Cuba. President Kennedy was also credited for helping put man on the moon and promoting civil rights.

The Cuban Missile Crisis of 1962 is believed to have been the closest the world has come to World War III. The crisis came about as the result of the U.S. learning that the Soviet Union and the Communist nation of Cuba were building nuclear missile bases in Cuba. The U.S. promptly quarantined the island of Cuba and demanded that the Soviets dismantle the bases and remove any offensive weapons there. The Soviets countered by stating that any attempts by America to quarantine international waters would be an act of aggression that would lead to a nuclear war. The world feared the worst, but the conflict ended when the Soviets agreed to withdraw and the U.S. promised not to invade Cuba. The world sighed in relief.

76 ★ Meet the Chief

President Kennedy went to West Berlin in 1963 and delivered a speech condemning the Soviet Union for building the Berlin Wall. The wall (a mass of concrete and barbed wire that separated Communist East Berlin from non-Communist West Berlin) was built to stop Germans caught in the Soviet-controlled areas from fleeing to the non-Communist world. Despite the president's visit, the wall stayed erected and divided some families for several decades to come. It wasn't until 1989 (following the collapse of the Soviet Union) that the gates in the wall were opened to allow Germans from both sides to reunite.

President Kennedy with wife Jackie in the limousine in Dallas, Texas, on Main Street, minutes before the assassination

Tragically, while he was in Dallas, Texas, campaigning to be re-elected, Kennedy was shot and killed by Lee Harvey Oswald. The nation mourned its loss.

President John F. Kennedy (center right, standing at microphones) delivering remarks at Free University of Berlin in West Berlin, West Germany (Federal Republic)

"I believe in an America where religious intolerance will someday end–where all men and all churches are treated as equal–where every man has the same right to attend or not attend the church of his choice.
—John F. Kennedy[37]"

Approximately 5,000 people escaped to West Berlin when the Berlin Wall was in use and nearly 200 were killed trying. Some escaped by digging tunnels under the wall, others drove through security check points under a hail of bullet fire, and a few flew hot air balloons and ultralights over the barrier.

#35 John F. Kennedy ★ 77

sample spread

The Presidential Oath

I do solemnly swear that I will faithfully execute the office of the President of the United States, and will, to the best of my ability, preserve, protect, and defend the Constitution of the United States.

A note about our presidents

Each president is unique in their faith and beliefs. As you learn more about the presidents of the United States, you may find that not all of them followed godly or biblical principles; they made mistakes, as well as accomplished great things. We hope as you learn about each president, you will be inspired to learn more about them and America, and will think of ways you might contribute to this great nation. Maybe one day you will become the president of the United States of America!

White House press briefing room

President Trivia Games

Who Am I?
2001-2009
See page 92

Trivia: Who was the second president of the United States?
See page 10

Two trivia games in one!

Turn to any president's page and look for the President Trivia Games at the top. Choose whether you want to guess who the president is in the picture, with his dates as president, or if you want to answer the trivia question. You can just do one or two at a time, or go through the whole book from beginning to end to see how many you know!

Index of the Presidents

George Washington

#1

1789–1797

Independent

Born: February 22, 1732

Died: December 14, 1799

1788–1789

- ☆ George Washington is elected America's first president
- ☆ Washington sworn in as America's first president

George Washington was born in Virginia when Virginia was still an English colony. When he was young, Washington became a surveyor and a soldier in the English army. Over time, he (like many colonists) became tired of being ruled by a king and wanted America to be independent.

George Washington during his surveyor days

George Washington wearing his colonel's uniform of the Virginia Regiment from the French and Indian War

On July 9, 1776, Washington led an American Independence celebration in New York City, reading the Declaration of Independence to the troops and sending copies of it to generals in the Continental Army.

When the colonies finally decided to break free from English rule, Washington (who was general of the Continental Army) was chosen to lead the cause. The ensuing war was tough and lasted seven years, but through General Washington's leadership, the colonists won their freedom in 1783.

Though Washington became a hero, he didn't try to capitalize on his popularity. Instead, he returned to his farm in Virginia. A few years later, however, his country needed his services one more time. His country needed a president!

George Washington and the Continental Army crossing the Delaware River during the Revolutionary War

1790

- ☆ The U.S. capital is moved from New York City to Philadelphia
- ☆ Bill of Rights adopted, ensuring freedom of religion

1796–1797

- ☆ America takes control of Detroit from the British
- ☆ Washington retires to Virginia after serving his last term

President Trivia Games

Who Am I?
1801–1809

See page 12

Trivia: Who was president during the Civil War?

See page 38

General George Washington Resigning His Commission

George Washington is often called the "father" of our country. He is one of the four presidents featured on Mount Rushmore.

After the U.S. Constitution became the law of the land, Americans needed to select a president that they could trust, and they chose George Washington. President Washington served four years and was re-elected for a second term. After his second term ended, he returned to his home in Virginia.

John Adams was Washington's chief opponent in both elections. In those days, Adams became America's vice president because he received the second most votes.

George Washington died peacefully on December 14, 1799, from complications of an infection during a cold winter.

Scene at the Signing of the Constitution of the United States

> *For happily the Government of the United States, which gives to bigotry no sanction, to persecution no assistance requires only that they who live under its protection should demean themselves as good citizens, in giving it on all occasions their effectual support.*
>
> —George Washington[1]

John Adams

1797–1801

#2

Federalist

Born: October 30, 1735

Died: July 4, 1826

1797

- ☆ John Adams takes office as new president
- ☆ *Old Ironsides* sets sail to defend America

Birthplace of President John Adams, in Quincy, Massachusetts

John Adams, the oldest of three sons, was born in 1735 in what is now Quincy, Massachusetts. At the age of 16 he went to Harvard College. He became a schoolteacher after he graduated and then a successful lawyer. In 1764, he married Abigail Smith and they had six children.

In 1770, John Adams became the lawyer for a number of British soldiers who were being tried for murder after they fired upon American colonists in what is called the Boston Massacre, which led to the deaths of five colonists. Despite local anger toward the soldiers, Adams saved all the men on trial from the hangman's rope. Hard feelings for Adams didn't last long because, a few years later, Massachusetts chose him as one of its representatives to the First and Second Continental Congresses!

John Adams served as George Washington's vice president during Washington's two terms. When Washington retired, the country cast ballots for a new president, and Adams was its pick. Shortly after Adams took office, our nation was thrust into a "quasi-war" with France.

By 1796, France and Great Britain were engaged in a war that had been going on for nearly ten years. France began capturing American ships because France saw America as a British ally. Neither the U.S. nor France ever officially declared war on the other. President Adams and many U.S. leaders feared a French invasion and built up the army and navy, but France didn't attack American soil and the United States remained safe.

Did you know that John Adams is considered one of America's Founding Fathers? In 1776, he was the foremost debater in trying to get the Declaration of Independence adopted by the Continental Congress . . . and he signed it too!

The Boston Massacre as portrayed by Paul Revere

1799

- ☆ In France, Napoleon overthrows his nation's Executive Directory
- ☆ George Washington dies in Virginia

1800

- ☆ The first vaccination in the U.S. against smallpox is administered
- ☆ The U.S. Census counts 5.3 million Americans

President Trivia Games

Who Am I?
1961–1963
See page 76

Trivia: Who was the first African American president?
See page 94

Declaration of Independence being presented to the Congress. John Adams is the man in center with his hands on his hips.

The USS *Constitution* (or *Old Ironsides*) was christened on October 21, 1797, when John Adams was president. The 44-gun, three-masted frigate would sail into history, defeating five British warships in the War of 1812. Today, the USS *Constitution* is still officially on active duty, easily making the ship the oldest commissioned vessel in the U.S. Navy.

The earliest known depiction of USS *Constitution*

> *Now I will avow, that I then believe, and now believe, that those general Principles of Christianity, are as eternal and immutable, as the Existence and Attributes of God.*
>
> —John Adams[7]

Thomas Jefferson

#3

1801–1809

Democratic-Republican

Born: April 13, 1743

Died: July 4, 1826

1801

☆ Thomas Jefferson takes office as new president

☆ The First Barbary War begins

☆ The Cane Ridge, Kentucky, Camp Meeting

Jefferson was the designing architect of his home, Monticello, in Virginia

Jefferson became the primary author of the Declaration of Independence. The document was written in 1776 and stated that the 13 colonies were finished with being ruled by the British and were now free to govern as they pleased. Of course, England was outraged with the colonists, and the Revolutionary War soon began.

Map of the United States with the Louisiana Purchase highlighted (in white)

Thomas Jefferson was born in 1743 in Virginia. He was the third of ten children. When he was 14 years old, his father died, and young Thomas inherited 5,000 acres of land and dozens of slaves. In 1772, he married Martha Wayles Skelton. The two had six children together. Tragically, one child died at birth.

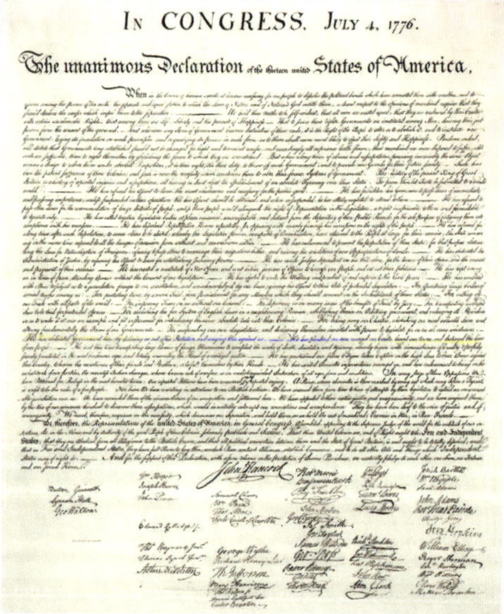

In Congress, July 4, 1776.

The unanimous Declaration of the thirteen united States of America,

The United States Declaration of Independence

In the election of 1800, Jefferson's political party was so confident of victory over President John Adams that it selected two candidates to run (Thomas Jefferson and Aaron Burr). But when the votes were cast and the electoral college met to select a winner, the unthinkable happened. Jefferson and Burr were tied with 73 votes each! According to the Constitution, if there was a tie, the U.S. House of Representatives would have to meet and vote for a winner. And vote they did! Thirty-five times the House voted, and each time Jefferson and Burr got the same number of votes. Finally, in the 36th vote, Federalist Alexander Hamilton broke party ranks and cast the deciding vote for Jefferson. Jefferson

1803–1804

☆ The U.S. makes the Louisiana Purchase from France

☆ Ohio becomes the 17th state

1805

☆ Lewis and Clark begin their exploration of the West

President Trivia Games

Who Am I?
2009–2017
See page 94

Trivia: Which president was assassinated in Dallas, Texas?
See page 76

became president and, thanks to Hamilton, Aaron Burr had to settle with being vice president. This became one of the most disputed elections in history.

In 1804, Aaron Burr and Alexander Hamilton dueled each other in New Jersey. Hamilton shot first and missed. Burr, who was still vice president at the time, returned fire. His musket ball struck Hamilton in the lower abdomen and, a few moments later, Hamilton died. The duel stemmed from the 1800 presidential election and was legal at that time.

Four years later, he was elected to a second term. During Jefferson's presidency, the U.S. made the Louisiana Purchase from France. The United States nearly doubled in size when it made the Louisiana Purchase from France for 15 million dollars. Over time, the United States would expand to reach the Pacific coast. Jefferson retired after his second term ended in 1809.

Duel between Alexander Hamilton and Aaron Burr

Did you know that Thomas Jefferson and John Adams died on the same day? The date was July 4, 1826.

Jefferson Memorial in Washington, D.C.

> *God who gave us life gave us liberty.*
> *And can the liberties of a nation be thought secure*
> *when we have removed their only firm basis,*
> *a conviction in the minds of the people*
> *that these liberties are of the Gift of God?*
>
> —Thomas Jefferson[3]

James Madison

#4

1809–1817

Democratic-Republican

Born: March 16, 1751

Died: June 28, 1836

1809–1810

- ☆ James Madison takes office
- ☆ The U.S. Census counts 7.2 million Americans

Madison wrote the Constitution at his estate near Orange, Virginia, called Montpelier.

James Madison, the oldest of 12 children, was born in Virginia in 1751. In his youth, he studied under a Scottish teacher and a reverend. In 1769, he began studies at what is now Princeton University and graduated two years later. Madison was only 25 years old when the Revolutionary War began. He served in the Virginia state legislature for most of the war and became a friend of Thomas Jefferson.

Congress of the United States

The Bill of Rights, twelve articles of amendment to the to the United States Constitution proposed in 1789

After the Revolutionary War, Madison became more active as an American politician and political philosopher. He was the principal author of the U.S. Constitution and a key architect of the Bill of Rights. Because of this, he is often called both the "Father of the Constitution" and the "Father of the Bill of Rights."

Madison's work was appreciated by many, and he was chosen by President Jefferson to be America's secretary of state. He served in this position until the end of Jefferson's final term in office, and his popularity continued to grow.

The capture of USS *President* was the last naval duel to take place during the War of 1812.

After Jefferson retired, James Madison ran for president in 1808 and won. He also won again four years later. During his tenure as commander in chief, he had to deal with one of the most trying times in U.S. history, the War of 1812. Battles against the British were fought in Canada, the Atlantic Ocean, the Gulf of Mexico, and on American soil.

The War of 1812 is also known as America's second war of independence with the British

1812–1813

- ☆ The War of 1812 begins
- ☆ James Madison begins his second term as war continues

1814–1815

- ☆ Washington, D.C., is captured and burned by the British
- ☆ America wins the War of 1812

President Trivia Games

Who Am I?
1913–1921
See page 62

Trivia: Who was elected president a record four times?
See page 70

Empire. Francis Scott Key penned the words to the American National Anthem during this war. The war officially began with an American declaration. Why were the Americans upset? First, Britain introduced trade restrictions that impeded American trade with France. Secondly, Britain began forcing American citizens to serve in the Royal Navy. Finally, Britain began supporting American Indians who were attacking American settlers in what are now Ohio, Indiana, Illinois, Michigan, and Wisconsin.

American soldiers in civilian clothes take on the British in the Battle of New Orleans.

The British Burning Washington

Did you know that the Battle of New Orleans took place after the war was over? Due to poor means of communication, the commanders on both sides didn't receive news of the war's end until after the battle was fought!

The British struck a huge blow during the war by invading Washington, D.C., and burning the White House to the ground. The U.S. countered by successfully defending Baltimore and routing the English at the Battle of New Orleans. In the end, the United States won the war, and Britain realized it would never regain control of its old colonies. In the end, President Madison led the U.S. to victory and put an end to England's threat of taking over the country. He retired after his second term ended.

> *The belief in a God All Powerful wise and good, is so essential to the moral order of the world and to the happiness of man, that arguments which enforce it cannot be drawn from too many sources.*
>
> —James Madison[4]

James Monroe

#5

1817–1825

Democratic-Republican

Born: April 28, 1758

Died: July 4, 1831

1817–1818

- ☆ James Monroe takes office as new president
- ☆ In Canada, the 49th Parallel is set between the U.S. and Britain

James Monroe was born in Virginia in 1758. As a student, he excelled in many subjects. When he was 16, he enrolled in the College of William and Mary, but the atmosphere leading to the Revolutionary War compelled Monroe to quit his studies and fight for America's freedom.

The Capture of the Hessians at the Battle of Trenton. On the left, the severely wounded Lieutenant James Monroe is helped by Dr. John Riker.

Shortly after the battles of Lexington and Concord in June of 1775, Monroe joined 24 men and raided an arsenal where they took muskets and swords. He later joined the Continental Army and served with distinction at the Battle of Trenton. After the war, he studied law under Thomas Jefferson and married Elizabeth Kortright. As time passed, he became a leading candidate for the presidency.

Elizabeth Kortright Monroe, wife of James Monroe

With the Federalist Party in disarray, James Monroe became president by winning the elections of 1816 and 1820. In office, he began what is known as the "Monroe Doctrine," which stated that the U.S. would no longer tolerate European interference or colonization in both North and South America. The U.S. also purchased Florida from Spain for five million dollars, which, in turn, prompted war between America and the Seminole Indians living there. President Monroe retired after his second term ended.

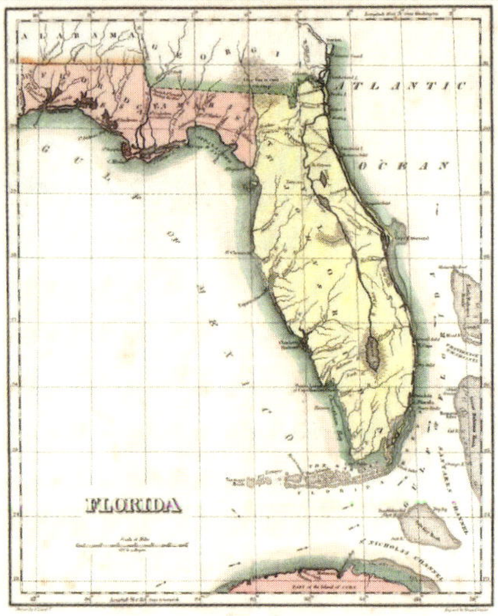

1822 map of Florida Territory, published less than a year after Florida was ceded to the U.S. by Spain

The United States saw its borders with neighboring nations better defined while James Monroe was president. In the northwest, the U.S. and Britain established the 49th parallel as the border between

1820

☆ The Missouri Compromise settles a slavery dispute in Congress

☆ The U.S. Census counts 9.6 million Americans

1821–1822

☆ Missouri becomes a state

☆ Florida becomes a U.S. territory

President Trivia Games

Who Am I?
1881–1881
See page 46

Trivia: Which president was the hero of the Battle of New Orleans?
See page 20

Canada (controlled by Great Britain at the time) and the Louisiana Purchase Territory (controlled by the U.S.). In the south, the U.S. expanded its borders by purchasing Florida from Spain in 1819. The U.S. also received territory in what is now southwestern Louisiana from the Spanish that same year.

A beach in Monrovia, the capital of Liberia

The American Colonization Society (ACS) was established in Washington, D.C., in 1816 for the purpose of returning freed African American slaves to Africa. It was founded by a small group of men, including Paul Cuffee, who captained voyages to Sierra Leone where he helped some African Americans establish a new colony.

The colony of Freetown in Sierra Leone

In 1821, the society began transporting more freed African Americans to other areas along Africa's west coast. With the help of the ACS, these new colonists pulled together, grew in power, and founded the Republic of Liberia. Without a doubt this new nation was unique to Africa. It modeled its government similar to that of the United States and even named its capital Monrovia, in honor of President James Monroe, who supported Liberia's existence.

> *Our country may be likened to a new house. We lack many things, but we possess the most precious of all — liberty!*
>
> —James Monroe[5]

John Quincy Adams

#6

1825–1829

Democratic-Republican

Born: July 11, 1767

Died: February 23, 1848

1825–1826

- ☆ John Quincy Adams takes office
- ☆ The Erie Canal is opened in New York
- ☆ America's first railroad is chartered in Massachusetts

John Quincy Adams' wife, Louisa Adams

John Quincy Adams was born in 1767 in Massachusetts. He was the son of John Adams, the second president of the United States. When John Quincy was young, he spent much of his time in France and the Netherlands with his father, who was on diplomatic missions. During this time, he mastered the French and Dutch languages.

In 1797, John Quincy was appointed as minister to Prussia. While in London, he married Louisa Johnson, the daughter of an American merchant. He returned to America and was elected to the Massachusetts State Senate, appointed as the first ever U.S. Minister to Russia, and negotiated the Treaty of Ghent, which ended the War of 1812. He was certainly a man on the move, and he ran for president in 1824.

John Quincy Adams didn't receive the most popular votes or electoral votes in the election of 1824, but he was elected by the House of Representatives to be the next president anyway! Many of his opponents were supporters of Andrew Jackson (who had the most popular and electoral votes) and they felt robbed. So they did almost everything they could to keep President Adams from succeeding while he was in office. When the next election came around, President Adams was defeated by (you guessed it!) Andrew Jackson.

The election of 1824 was unique and featured four strong candidates for president. The initial electoral count had Andrew Jackson in the lead with 99 electoral votes, Adams was second with 84 votes, William Crawford had 41, and Henry Clay had 37. Now, because Andrew Jackson didn't carry more than 50% of the total electoral votes (he needed at

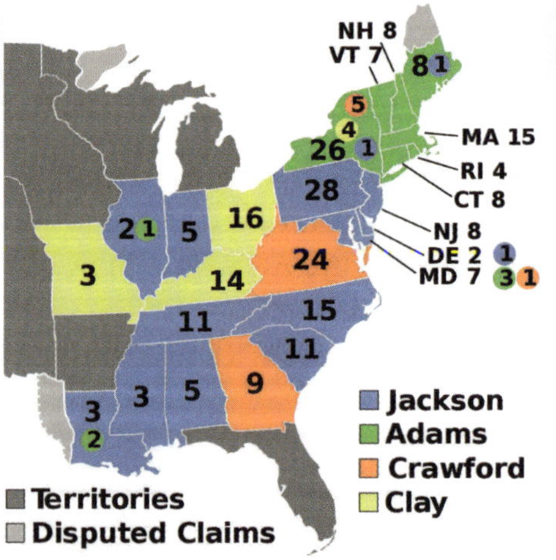

1824 electoral map

1827

- ☆ America's first African-American newspaper is founded
- ☆ New Orleans celebrates its first Mardi Gras
- ☆ The Baltimore and Ohio Railroad is incorporated

1828

- ☆ Noah Webster publishes his new dictionary
- ☆ The first Native American newspaper, The *Cherokee Phoenix*, is printed

President Trivia Games

Who Am I?
1837–1841
See page 22

Trivia: Who was president when abolitionist John Brown was hanged?
See page 36

least 131), it was left to the House of Representatives to determine who would be the next president. The House met to decide the matter, voted, and elected John Quincy Adams to be the next president. Andrew Jackson was understandably in shock with this outcome, and America got a strange lesson in the presidential election process.

Signing of the Treaty of Ghent

Secretary of State Henry Clay

Noah Webster published his *An American Dictionary of the English Language* in 1828, and it was no easy task. He began work on the project in 1807 and learned a staggering 26 languages to bolster his etymology of words!

When the House of Representatives met to consider who would be the next president following the 1824 election, only the top three candidates could be considered. As a result, Henry Clay wasn't on the ballot. Still, Clay had a tremendous impact on the election's outcome because he was speaker of the House of Representatives. From his position, Clay used his power of persuasion to steer voters away from Jackson (whom Clay didn't like) and to Adams, the eventual winner. William Crawford was also on the ballot, but he didn't pose a threat to either Adams or Jackson.

> *In the chain of human events, the birthday of the nation is indissolubly linked with the birthday of the Savior. The Declaration of Independence laid the cornerstone of human government upon the first precepts of Christianity.*
>
> —John Quincy Adams[6]

Andrew Jackson

1829–1837

Democrat

Born: March 15, 1767

Died: June 8, 1845

#7

1829–1830

- ☆ Andrew Jackson takes office
- ☆ The Indian Removal Act is passed
- ☆ The U.S. Census counts 12.8 million Americans

Young Jackson refusing to clean Major Coffin's boots

Andrew Jackson was born in South Carolina in 1767. At the age of 13, he was imprisoned by the British during the Revolutionary War and nearly starved to death. One soldier even slashed Jackson with a sword when Jackson refused to shine the soldier's boots! Years after the war, Jackson became a lawyer and settled in Tennessee.

Before the turn of the century, Jackson became a U.S. Representative and then a U.S. senator for Tennessee, but his actions in the War of 1812 threw him into the spotlight. After defeating Tecumseh, a Shawnee chief, and being promoted to Major General, he took charge of the American defenses at New Orleans and, with only 5,000 men, defeated 7,500 British troops. Andrew Jackson became a hero and decided to run for the presidency.

Andrew Jackson's home, The Hermitage, near Nashville, Tennessee

Andrew Jackson lost the presidential election of 1824 despite having the most popular votes, but he came back to win the elections of 1828 and 1832. In office, President Jackson tried and failed to get Congress to abolish the Electoral College. He also removed many Indian tribes from their lands and forced them to move farther west. After his second term ended, President Jackson retired to "The Hermitage," his Tennessee estate.

Tomb of Andrew and Rachel Jackson in the garden of The Hermitage

It is interesting to note something that happened after the battle of Tallushatchee. Some soldiers found an infant Native American boy with his dead mother, and because none of the captives wanted to care for the child, and perhaps because Jackson had been orphaned himself at 14, he sent the child to be cared for. When he returned home he named

1831–1832

- ☆ Nat Turner leads a slave uprising in Virginia and fails
- ☆ The U.S. intensifies its war against American Indians

1834–1835

- ☆ Congress creates Oklahoma as an Indian territory
- ☆ Slaves from Florida revolt and join the Seminole Indians

President Trivia Games

Who Am I?
1945–1953
See page 72

Trivia: Which president was dumped by his own party in 1856?
See page 34

the child Lincoyer and raised him as his own. Lincoyer grew up knowing his heritage, as visitors from the Creek nation that he was a part of would visit Jackson at the Hermitage. Sadly, the young man died of tuberculosis while still a teen.

> *When I have Suffered sufficiently, the Lord will then take me to himself, but what are all my sufferings compared to those of the blessed Saviour, who died upon that cursed tree for me, mine are nothing.*
>
> —Andrew Jackson[7]

During the War of 1812, Andrew Jackson became a hero by leading U.S. forces to victory at the Battle of New Orleans.

Martin Van Buren

#8

1837–1841

Democrat

Born: December 5, 1782

Died: July 24, 1862

1837

- ☆ Martin Van Buren takes office
- ☆ The Panic of 1837 leads to bank runs and food riots
- ☆ Michigan is admitted as the 26th U.S. state

The birthplace of President Martin Van Buren in Kinderhook, New York

Martin Van Buren was born in 1782 in New York. Because all previous presidents were born prior to 1776, he was the first one to be "born" an American citizen. He began studying law at the young age of 14 and became a lawyer when he was 20. In 1807, he married Hannah Hoes, his childhood sweetheart.

Van Buren's wealth grew with his law practice, and he soon became active in politics. He was elected a U.S. senator from New York in 1821 and, a few years later, became the state's governor. But his stint as governor didn't last long. Two months after taking office, he accepted President Jackson's offer to become secretary of state. Then, during Jackson's second term, Van Buren became President Jackson's vice president.

Hannah Van Buren

An 1837 caricature about Balaam's donkey placing the blame for the Panic of 1837 on Andrew Jackson and Martin Van Buren

Martin Van Buren became president after winning the election of 1836. Upon taking office, he retained nearly all of President Jackson's cabinet members. During his term, he angered many when he denied Texas its request to join the United States. He also was blamed for the economic turmoil stemming from the Panic of 1837 and a commercial crisis, which began a year later. Because of these troubled times, he was labeled Martin Van "Ruin" and failed in his re-election attempt.

The inhabitants of Texas (many of whom were American settlers) won their independence from Mexico in 1836 and tried to join the United States a year later. President Van Buren blocked this from happening, partly because he wanted America to stay at peace with Mexico. As a result, Texas stood alone as its own country for a while. That's right, its own country!

1838

☆ Samuel Morse demonstrates the telegraph

☆ Frederick Douglass escapes from slavery

1839

☆ Dueling is outlawed in Washington, D.C.

☆ The Liberty Party forms in opposition to slavery

President Trivia Games

Who Am I?
1857–1861
See page 36

Trivia: Who was the president during the Mexican-American War?
See page 28

Richard Mentor Johnson was the ninth vice president of the United States.

Beginning in 1838, Van Buren ordered soldiers to force over 15,000 Native Americans from their homes, making them march about 1,200 miles to the Oklahoma Territory. A fourth of the people died along the way. This forced removal was based on a policy established by Andrew Jackson of moving Native people farther west.

The *Amistad* Revolt

When slaves took over the Cuban ship *Amistad* and ended up in the United States, President Van Buren sided with the Spanish government that wanted all the slaves returned to its custody as runaways. However, the Supreme Court had the final say in the matter and allowed the slaves to freely return to Africa. After the Supreme Court's decision, the freed Africans set sail for home.

> *From a small community we have risen*
> *to a people powerful in numbers and in strength;*
> *but with our increase has gone hand*
> *in hand the progress of just principles.*
>
> —Martin Van Buren[8]

William H. Harrison

#9

1841–1841

Whig

Born: February 9, 1773

Died: April 4, 1841

1841

☆ President Harrison delivers the longest inaugural address

☆ President Harrison receives many White House visitors

☆ Cornstarch is patented

William Henry Harrison was born in 1773 in Virginia. He was the youngest of seven children and the last president to be born a British subject. Harrison joined the U.S. Army when he was 18 and fought Indians at the Battle of Fallen Timbers in 1794. He married Anna Symmes and the two had ten children together.

William Henry Harrison, congressional delegate from the Northwest Territory in 1800

Harrison resigned from the military in 1797 and was appointed Secretary of the Northwest Territory. In the following years, he fought for the rights of many settlers in the area and became the first governor of the Indiana Territory. Strangely enough, while holding this political position, Harrison led U.S. troops to defeat Indians at the battle of Tippecanoe. This victory made Harrison a popular man.

Riding his popularity, Harrison won the presidential election of 1840 and took the oath of office on March 4, 1841. On that cold and rainy day, he stood outside and delivered the longest inaugural address in U.S. history. He then rode in a parade. Sadly, President Harrison developed pneumonia on March 26 and died from its complications a few weeks later. In the end, President Harrison was the first president to die in office and a question was raised as to whether the vice president could indeed become the next president! The answer was yes, he could.

While William Henry Harrison was governor of the Indiana Territory, white settlers were encroaching upon Native American lands illegally. To counter this, Shawnee chieftain Tecumseh launched a movement among the Shawnees and other local tribes that attempted to unite the Indians and prevent further expansion of white settlers into their territories. His confederation of tribes built

The Road to Fallen Timbers, the Legion of the United States makes contact with the Western Confederacy.

1841

☆ President Harrison refuses to dismiss many Democrat appointees

☆ President Harrison becomes ill

1841

☆ President Harrison develops pneumonia

☆ President Harrison dies and Vice President John Tyler is sworn in

President Trivia Games

Who Am I?
1849–1850
See page 30

Trivia: Which president sent Commodore Perry to Japan?
See page 32

a settlement where the Wabash and Tippecanoe rivers met, and this settlement became a focal point of Tecumseh's movement. On November 7, 1881, Harrison took 1,100 men to this settlement and battled the Shawnees (minus Tecumseh, who was away recruiting). Though the actual battle was considered a draw by most historians, its aftermath favored Harrison. Many Shawnees lost the desire to remain united, and Harrison was seen as a hero.

The William Henry Harrison Memorial in North Bend, Ohio

Did you know that someone can't catch a cold by just standing in the rain or cold? The illness can only be contracted by coming into contact with someone who is carrying the virus. So, contrary to what you may have heard, President Harrison's standing in the cold rain didn't cause him to die.

Harrison's 32 days in office marked the shortest tenure of all the presidents.

> *I deem the present occasion sufficiently important and solemn to justify me in expressing to my fellow-citizens a profound reverence for the Christian religion and a thorough conviction that sound morals, religious liberty, and a just sense of religious responsibility are essentially connected with all true and lasting happiness.*
>
> —William H. Harrison[9]

General William H. Harrison, at the Battle of Tippecanoe

John Tyler

#10

1841–1845

Whig

Born: March 29, 1790

Died: January 18, 1862

1841

- ☆ John Tyler becomes president after Harrison dies
- ☆ Wagon trains begin leaving Missouri for California
- ☆ The *Amistad* survivors return to Africa to be free

Tyler's birthplace, Greenway Plantation in Charles City County, Virginia

John Tyler was born in Virginia in 1790 and received a quality education. At the age of 12, he entered a prep school. He entered college three years later and graduated when he was only 17 years old. By the age of 20, Tyler was a lawyer! When the War of 1812 began, he joined a militia to fight against the British.

After the war, Tyler began his political career at the state level in Virginia. He became a U.S. representative in 1816 and a U.S. senator in 1827. In 1836, he ran as a vice-presidential candidate for the Whig party, but the ticket came in third place in the general election. Four years later, in 1840, he once again became his party's choice for vice president with William Henry Harrison heading the ticket. Together, Harrison and Tyler won the election and John Tyler became America's new vice president.

Tyler receiving news of Harrison's death

John Tyler became president following the death of President Harrison in 1841, becoming the first president not to be elected. During his term, he upset members of his party (the Whigs) by practically vetoing every bill that crossed his desk. In fact, after having vetoed one bill, the Whigs changed its wording to meet President Tyler's approval and he vetoed it again! The Whigs were enraged and, as a result, expelled President Tyler from their party. When it came time for the next election, the Whigs chose Henry Clay as its nominee, and President Tyler didn't run. Instead, he threw his support to James K. Polk, a Democrat.

American forces repelled a British assault on New Orleans in January 1815.

The first electric telegraph message was sent on May 1, 1844, saying that Henry Clay was the Whig Party's nominee.

1842–1843

- ☆ The sewing machine is patented
- ☆ The typewriter is patented

1844–1845

- ☆ The first telegraph line is completed
- ☆ Goodyear patents vulcanization of rubber
- ☆ Edgar Allen Poe's "Raven" is published

President Trivia Games

Who Am I?
1850–1853
See page 34

Trivia: "Old Rough and Ready" was this president's nickname.
See page 30

Breaking up Camp at Sunrise, wagon train on the Oregon Trail

Several years before John Tyler became president, the American economy was so bad that many Americans either lost their jobs or saw their wages cut by as much as 50%. People were suffering and looking for a better life. One small group of 70 people believed they would find prosperity in the West, so they departed Missouri in wagons in 1841. Not long afterward, more and more Americans followed this group's lead and traveled in wagon trains to the Oregon and California territories. Many of them were led by promises of rich soil and paradise. Sadly, what most found when they reached their destinations was anything but. The land was untamed, supplies were scarce, and the threat of being robbed or killed was high.

The Oregon Trail, the Santa Fe Trail, and the Mormon Trail were a few of the routes wagon trains used to go west. It's believed that nearly 400,000 Americans traveled along these trails between 1841 and 1866.

> *Wealth can only be accumulated by the earnings of industry and the savings of frugality.*
>
> —John Tyler[10]

James K. Polk

#11

1845–1849

Democrat

Born: November 2, 1795

Died: June 15, 1849

1846–1847

- ☆ The Mexican-American War begins after Texas becomes a state
- ☆ The U.S. Marines capture Mexico City

James K. Polk was born in North Carolina in 1795. In 1806, he moved with his family to Tennessee. Polk suffered from poor health and had to have an operation to remove urinary stones when he was 16 years old. This surgery took place in Kentucky.

Reconstruction of the log cabin in Pineville, North Carolina, where Polk was born

While attending the University of North Carolina, Polk took part in debates and learned the art of oratory. After graduating, he studied law in Nashville, became popular, and began his political career. Polk was elected to the Tennessee state legislature in 1823, became a U.S. Representative in 1825, and served as Tennessee's governor from 1839 to 1841. In 1844, he ran for president.

James K. Polk won the election of 1844 and promised to serve only one term. In office, he annexed Texas into the Union, knowing that this would anger Mexico. He also expanded U.S. boundaries by acquiring the Oregon Territory through negotiations with Great Britain and territories in the Southwest after having a "small" war with Mexico. True to his word, after his term drew to a close, he didn't pursue being re-elected. He went into retirement after leaving office.

The Mexican-American War lasted from 1846 to 1848 and was the result of the U.S. admitting Texas to the Union as a state. During the war, American forces seized large parts of northern Mexico, blockaded the Mexican coast, and invaded Mexico City. After its capital was captured, the Mexican government was left with few options and was ready to make peace on U.S. terms. The Treaty of Guadalupe Hidalgo was signed by both sides and the war ended. As part of this treaty, Mexico gave up its claim to Texas and sold what are now the American states of California, Nevada, Utah, and Arizona.

1844 campaign banner for the Polk/Dallas ticket

1848

☆ Chinese immigrants begin arriving in San Francisco

☆ The Mexican-American War comes to an end

☆ Gas lights are installed in the White House

1849

☆ Elizabeth Blackwell becomes America's first female doctor

President Trivia Games

Who Am I?
1853–1857
See page 32

Trivia: Who beat Samuel Tilden in the election of 1876?
See page 44

Many Americans who fought during the Mexican-American War became famous in the coming years. Zachary Taylor was a general and became president of the United States. Winfield Scott was also a general and grew to legendary status as both a military strategist and commander. Ulysses S. Grant, George B. McClellan, Ambrose Burnside, Robert E. Lee, James Longstreet, "Stonewall" Jackson, and George Meade served as junior officers in Mexico and became household names as military leaders during the Civil War. And Jefferson Davis became the president of the Confederacy during the Civil War.

James K. Polk's tomb lies on the grounds of the Tennessee State Capitol.

On the other side of the conflict, Mexico's General Santa Anna succeeded in becoming his country's president in 1853. He was later forced from office, declared a traitor, and lived in various parts of the world including Cuba and the United States. He was allowed to return to Mexico in 1874 and died two years later.

> *One great object of the Constitution was to restrain majorities from oppressing minorities or encroaching upon their just rights.*
>
> —James K. Polk[11]

Zachary Taylor

#12

1849–1850

Whig

Born: November 24, 1784

Died: July 9, 1850

1849

- ☆ Zachary Taylor takes office
- ☆ Abraham Lincoln gets his first patent
- ☆ A gas mask is patented
- ☆ Gold is discovered in California

Zachary Taylor was born in 1784 in Virginia. He spent much of his youth in the Kentucky frontier and received tutoring whenever his father could find someone able. In 1808, Taylor joined the army. He fought in the Indiana Territory during the War of 1812 and against the Seminole Indians in Florida. Later, he went to Texas after it became a state.

General Taylor at the Battle of Resaca de la Palma

"An Available Candidate: The One Qualification for a Whig President." Political cartoon about the 1848 presidential election

In Texas, Taylor fought against Mexico during the Mexican-American War and became a hero after winning several battles where he was outnumbered. After the war, in 1848, he became the Whig Party's candidate for president despite him being a Southern slave owner at a time when many Southern states were ready to secede from the Union.

Taylor/Fillmore 1848 campaign poster

Zachary Taylor won the election of 1848. When he took office as the nation's 12th president, the question of whether or not slavery should be allowed in the new Western Territories was a hot topic. Despite being a slave owner himself, he angered many Southerners when he urged anti-slave territories in what are now Utah, New Mexico, and California to seek statehood quickly.

Zachary Taylor had an interesting family that clearly illustrates the divisions that the future Civil War would bring to many Americans. His son Richard served as a Confederate lieutenant general during the Civil War, and his daughter Sarah married future Confederate president Jefferson Davis in 1835. Sarah died of malaria three months after her marriage. In contrast to Richard, President Taylor's brother, Joseph Pannill Taylor, served as a brigadier general in the Union Army during the Civil War.

1850

☆ The city of San Francisco is incorporated

☆ The U.S. Census counts 23.1 million Americans

1850

☆ America's first female medical school opens

☆ President Taylor dies

President Trivia Games

Who Am I?
1897–1901
See page 56

Trivia: Who owned a newspaper in Ohio before becoming president?
See page 64

It is believed President Taylor died of acute gastroenteritis on July 9, 1850, after he consumed large amounts of cherries and milk during July fourth festivities held in Washington, D.C. After he became ill, his doctors gave him calomel, opium, and various other "healing" drugs of the time, and drained some of his blood. In hindsight, these acts to save the president's life most likely contributed to his untimely death. He was later buried near his parents' graves in Kentucky.

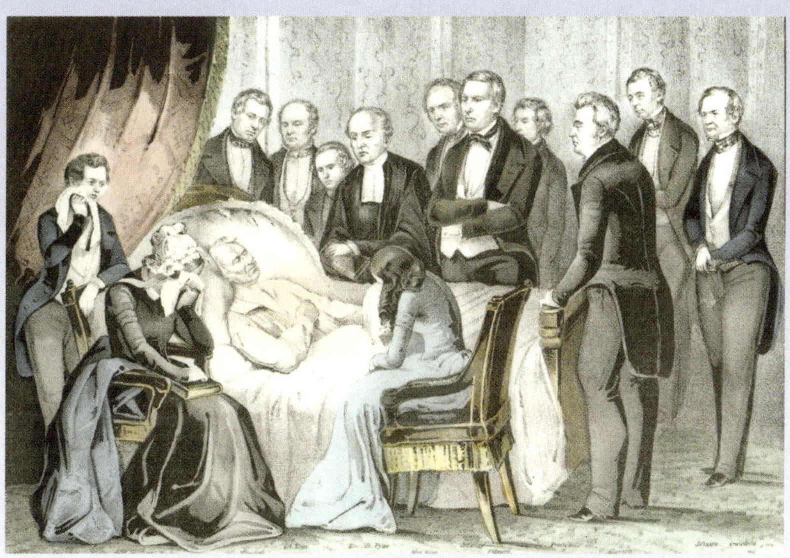

The death of Zachary Taylor

Zachary Taylor was known as "Old Rough and Ready" and served in the U.S. Army for 40 years prior to becoming president. During his lengthy military career, he fought in the War of 1812 against the British, as well as the Black Hawk War and the Second Seminole War against Native Americans. He also fought in the Mexican-American War where he became popular with many Americans.

> *I have always done my duty. I am ready to die. My only regret is for the friends I leave behind me.*
>
> —Zachary Taylor[12]

Millard Fillmore

#13

1850–1853

Whig

Born: January 7, 1800

Died: March 8, 1874

1850

- ☆ Millard Fillmore takes office
- ☆ The Great San Francisco Fire erupts in California
- ☆ Slave trade is no longer allowed in Washington, D.C.

Millard Fillmore was born in what was called the "frontier" of New York in 1800. He was born a few weeks after George Washington's death. Fillmore had a tough time obtaining an education due to the area's poor conditions, but when he was 19 he landed a job working for a judge and began studying law.

In the following years, Fillmore became a lawyer, married Abigail Powers, had two children, and entered politics. He held a state assembly position and later became a U.S. representative. In 1848, members of his party wanted a vice presidential candidate who could help them win the election. They chose Fillmore and the strategy worked. Zachary Taylor was elected president and Millard Fillmore became the vice president.

Andrew Jackson Donelson was on the Fillmore campaign ticket in 1856.

Millard Fillmore became president following President Zachary Taylor's death. In office, President Fillmore replaced members of the cabinet and tried to calm the slavery debate

Commodore Matthew C. Perry's visit to Kanagawa, Japan

1851

☆ Isaac Singer patents the sewing machine

☆ The telescope is patented by Alvan Clark

☆ Herman Melville's *Moby Dick* is published

1852

☆ Harriet Beecher Stowe's *Uncle Tom's Cabin* is published

☆ Ohio enacts child labor laws to protect children

President Trivia Games

Who Am I?
1889–1893
See page 52

Trivia: Who became president after William Henry Harrison died?
See page 26

between Northern and Southern states. The Fugitive Slave Law of 1850 led some abolitionists to create posters to warn African Americans to watch out! Another abolitionist, Harriet Beecher Stowe, told of slavery's horrors in her book *Uncle Tom's Cabin*. Many members of Fillmore's political party (the Whigs) became very upset with his policies, so they dropped President Fillmore and chose General Winfield Scott to represent them in the next election. Scott lost the 1852 presidential election, and the Whig Party began to fall apart.

Vice President Fillmore (upper right) presides over debates as Henry Clay takes the floor of the Old Senate Chamber.

Millard Fillmore gravesite at Forest Lawn Cemetery, Buffalo, New York

President Fillmore promoted American trade by sending Commodore Perry to Japan. When it opened its ports, Japan quickly developed into a modernized nation.

> *May God save the country,*
> *for it is evident the people will not.*
>
> —Millard Fillmore[13]

Franklin Pierce

1853–1857

Democrat

Born: November 23, 1804

Died: October 8, 1869

#14

1853

☆ Franklin Pierce takes office

☆ Harriet Tubman starts the "Underground Railroad"

☆ The Gadsden Purchase is made with Mexico

Jane Means Appleton Pierce

Franklin Pierce was born in a log cabin in New Hampshire in 1804. His family was poor, but Pierce was able to go to college where he graduated third in his class. He then completed law school and opened a practice in 1827. Several years later, he married Jane Appleton. They had three children. Sadly, all three died in childhood.

Pierce in his brigadier general's uniform

Pierce entered politics at the young age of 24 and held several positions in New Hampshire. When the Mexican-American War started in 1846, he postponed his political career and volunteered to fight. This decision nearly cost him his life. At the Battle of Contreras, Pierce's leg was seriously wounded. After it healed, he returned to New Hampshire to continue his political career and, in 1852, decided to run for president.

Franklin Pierce became president by winning the election of 1852. Before he took office, the debate over slavery was still a minor issue; however, shortly into his term, the passage of the Kansas-Nebraska Act (which repealed the Missouri Compromise) brought the question of slavery in the West to the forefront of national politics. To the public, President Pierce was perceived as a man who supported slavery.

Southerners feared they would soon be outnumbered in Congress and would no longer be able to keep African Americans in slavery. The passage of the Kansas-Nebraska Act in 1854 helped pacify these fears by allowing the peoples of territories in the West to decide if slavery would be allowed within their borders. A short time later, areas such as Kansas became hotbeds of violence when abolitionists clashed with those who wanted slavery.

In the 1856 presidential election, the Democratic Party dumped President Franklin Pierce, choosing

1854

- ☆ The first meeting of the Republican Party takes place
- ☆ Abraham Lincoln makes his first political speech

1856–1857

- ☆ Violence erupts in Kansas over the issue of slavery
- ☆ The Supreme Court rules that slaves can't be U.S. citizens

President Trivia Games

Who Am I?
1877–1881
See page 44

Trivia: Which president was a lieutenant general during the Civil War?
See page 42

instead to back James Buchanan for president. Four years later, the Democrats dumped Buchanan and extended their hands once again to Pierce. Pierce turned them down, thus paving the way for Abraham Lincoln to win.

Harriet Tubman escaped slavery in 1849 and, during Pierce's presidency, began a network called the "Underground Railroad" that helped other slaves escape. Aided by abolitionists who worked with her, Tubman helped thousands of runaway slaves reach Canada, Mexico, and Northern states where they could be free. Harriet Tubman became a hero and died in 1913 at the age of 93.

Harriet Tubman after the Civil War

1852 Democratic campaign banner for the Pierce/King ticket

> *I should shrink from a clear duty did I fail to express my deepest conviction that we can place no secure reliance upon any apparent progress if it be not sustained by national integrity, resting upon the great truths affirmed and illustrated by divine revelation.*
>
> —Franklin Pierce[14]

James Buchanan

#15

1857–1861

Democrat

Born: April 23, 1791

Died: June 1, 1868

1857

- ☆ James Buchanan takes office
- ☆ The first U.S. elevator is installed (in New York)

James Buchanan was born in 1791 in Pennsylvania. In college, he was expelled for poor behavior. He asked for a second chance and went on to graduate with honors. Afterward, he became a lawyer and fought in the War of 1812 where he helped defend Baltimore from the British. After the war, he turned his sights to a career in politics.

Buchanan became a U.S. representative in 1821 and was re-elected several times. Afterward, he wore many hats. He was the minister to Russia under President Jackson, the secretary of state under President Polk, and the minister to the court of St. James under President Pierce. When the 1856 presidential election came around, he was the Democratic Party's top pick for the presidency.

James Buchanan won the election of 1856 amid boiling tensions between Northern and Southern states over the issue of slavery. In office, he did little to cool these flames, and more and more people were ready to fight. When the next election came, the Democratic Party had a schism (between North and South, of course), and the Republicans won.

John C. Breckinridge, vice president of the United States under Buchanan

During President Buchanan's final days in the White House, he did little while the Southern states seceded from the Union, leaving Abraham Lincoln and the nation with a crisis.

John Brown was an abolitionist who increased tensions between Northern and Southern states during President Buchanan's term of office. After leading the Pottawatomie Massacre in Kansas in 1856, Brown returned east, raised some money, and made plans to raid the U.S. arsenal at Harper's

Buchanan memorial, Washington, D.C.

1858

- ☆ John Brown raids the arsenal at Harper's Ferry, Virginia
- ☆ The Trans-Atlantic Telegraph Cable is completed

1859–1860

- ☆ The first successful oil well is drilled (in Pennsylvania)
- ☆ Charles Darwin publishes *On the Origin of Species*
- ☆ The Pony Express begins delivering mail

President Trivia Games

Who Am I?
1865–1869
See page 40

Trivia: Which president was faced with the Panic of 1893 after taking office the second time?
See page 54

Ferry, Virginia. With barely 20 men, he hoped to secure the arsenal, seize weapons, and lead a slave revolt. His plan was launched on October 16, 1859, when he captured the arsenal, took hostages, and cut telegraph wires. However, the townspeople fought back and blocked Brown's escape route. Trapped for two days, Brown and his men were soon overwhelmed by U.S. Marines that President Buchanan dispatched and were captured. After a swift trial, Brown was found guilty and hanged for treason against the Commonwealth of Virginia. His death soon became a rallying cry for many opposed to slavery and warning of more deaths to come.

John Brown in 1859

Pony Express statue in St. Joseph, Missouri

In 1775, Benjamin Franklin served as the first postmaster of the postal service. However, there were always competitors that arose to try their hand at mail delivery.

In April of 1860, the Pony Express began making mail runs from Missouri to California. At that time, the most direct and fastest means of communication to the West was horseback. Conditions for the riders were harsh and many died when they encountered bad weather and hostile Indians along the 2,000-mile route.

> *What is right and what is practical are two different things.*
>
> —James Buchanan[15]

Abraham Lincoln

#16

1861–1865

Republican (1860) National Union (1864)

Born: February 12, 1809

Died: April 15, 1865

1861

☆ Abraham Lincoln takes office

☆ The Civil War begins with the siege of Fort Sumter

☆ To finance the war, the U.S. levies its first income tax

The farm site where Lincoln grew up in Spencer County, Indiana

Abraham Lincoln was born in a one-room log cabin in Kentucky in 1809. When he was seven years old, he moved with his family to Indiana. His mother died two years later. In 1830, his family moved to Illinois. Lincoln went to school for about 18 months in his youth, but he loved to read and, simply put, educated himself!

Despite lacking a formal education, Lincoln became a lawyer and, in 1846, a U.S. representative for the Whig party. He served one term in Congress and then resumed his law practice. In 1856, Lincoln helped organize a new political party, the Republican Party. Four years later, in 1860, he became its candidate for president. The self-educated Lincoln was ready for the White House.

Abraham Lincoln won the presidential election of 1860 and was re-elected in 1864. While in office, he was faced with the greatest crisis in American history — the Civil War. During his tenure, President Lincoln led the cause to preserve the Union, emancipated slaves in the Southern states, and witnessed hundreds of thousands of soldiers dying on both sides. In the end, President Lincoln helped win the war and the admiration of many people.

Lincoln with officers after the Battle of Antietam

1862–1863

- ☆ America introduces paper currency for the first time
- ☆ The fire extinguisher is patented
- ☆ Union forces win the Battle of Gettysburg

1865

- ☆ Confederate General Robert E. Lee surrenders
- ☆ President Lincoln is assassinated at Ford's Theater

President Trivia Games

Who Am I?
1797–1801
See page 10

Trivia: Who defeated John Adams in 1801 to become president?
See page 12

No doubt the Civil War was the most trying event of President Lincoln's administration and the nation. In fact, when Lincoln was sworn into office on March 3, 1861, the Confederacy (consisting of seven Southern states) was already established, having elected Jefferson Davis as its president. Several other states joined the Confederacy in the coming months and a devastating war ensued that lasted for four years. In the early stages of the war, the Confederate forces looked as if they might prevail in preserving the Confederacy. However, after numerous battles, the Union Army was able to force the Confederacy to surrender. The cost of the war was high, and not just in dollars. The Union lost nearly 360,000 men to battle and disease and the Confederacy lost roughly 260,000. The greatest benefit from the war was that slavery in the United States was ended.

John Wilkes Booth leaning to shoot President Abraham Lincoln

John Wilkes Booth shot President Lincoln in Ford's Theater in Washington, D.C., while the president was watching a play. Booth, an actor and a supporter of the Confederacy, ran from the scene but was later killed when Union forces tracked him to a farmhouse in Virginia. President Lincoln died shortly after the shooting.

Inauguration of Jefferson Davis as president of the Confederate States of America at Montgomery, Alabama

Abraham Lincoln is regarded as one of America's greatest presidents. His name and image appear in many places, including the five-dollar bill and penny.

> *'A house divided against itself cannot stand.' I believe this government cannot endure, permanently half slave and half free.*
>
> —Abraham Lincoln[16]

Andrew Johnson

1865–1869

National Union

Born: December 29, 1808

Died: July 31, 1875

#17

1865–1866

- ☆ Andrew Johnson takes office
- ☆ Slavery is abolished in the U.S.
- ☆ The Civil War is formally declared over
- ☆ Jesse James begins his robbery spree

Andrew Johnson was born in North Carolina in 1808. In his youth, he worked as a tailor and taught himself to read and write. He later moved to Tennessee and married Eliza McCradle. Johnson entered politics by becoming mayor of Greeneville and later was a U.S. representative.

The birthplace and first home of Andrew Johnson, Raleigh, North Carolina

Johnson became Tennessee's governor in 1853. Four years later, he was elected to the U.S. Senate. When the Civil War started, his state joined the Confederacy, but Johnson remained loyal to the Union. Because of this, he was thought to be the ideal candidate to run with Abraham Lincoln in 1864. The strategy worked. Lincoln won his re-election bid and Andrew Johnson became vice president.

Andrew Johnson became president after Lincoln's assassination, and his primary task in office was dealing with the Reconstruction of the Southern states that rebelled during the Civil War. He appointed leaders to govern the Southern states and ran into trouble when they began passing Black Codes that limited the freedoms of African Americans.

President Johnson upset many Republicans shortly after becoming president for a number of reasons. First, Johnson's policies toward the South were viewed as conciliatory in nature, and secondly, Johnson vetoed several civil rights bills that Republicans favored. For these reasons, a block of Republicans in the House of Representatives wanted the president removed from office. So, when they thought they had a chance, they impeached President Johnson, charging him for violating the Tenure of Office Act. The president was then tried before the Senate and found not guilty by one vote. If Johnson had been found guilty, he would have been removed from office. When the election of 1868 took place, President Johnson was so unpopular that he didn't get his party's endorsement. As a result, he dropped out of the race.

Eliza McCardle Johnson

1867

☆ The U.S. purchases Alaska from Russia

☆ First Reconstruction Act passed over Johnson's veto

1868–1869

☆ Many Southern states re-enter the Union

☆ Prosecutors drop treason case against Jefferson Davis

President Trivia Games

Who Am I?
1885–1889
1893–1897
See page 50

Trivia: Which president was the son of President John Adams?
See page 18

The Thirteenth Amendment to the Constitution abolished slavery and involuntary servitude (except as a punishment for a crime). It became the law of the land on December 6, 1865. Before becoming law, however, it was necessary for at least 75 percent of the 36 states existing at that time to approve the measure. So, when Georgia became the 27th state to give its approval, the amendment took effect nationwide. Slavery was officially abolished!

A Visit from the Old Mistress depicts a tense meeting between a group of newly freed slaves and their former slaveholder.

United States Republican 1864 presidential ticket

Though it was of no consequence, the nine "holdout" states did ratify the Thirteenth Amendment over time. Oregon, California, and Florida did so before the end of December 1865, and Iowa and New Jersey, the following year. Texas ratified the amendment in 1870 and Delaware waited until 1901. Remarkably, Kentucky didn't ratify the Thirteenth Amendment until 1976, and Mississippi, the last of the Civil War Era states, waited until 1995!

> *I have performed my duty to my God, my country, and my family. I have nothing to fear in approaching death. To me it is the mere shadow of God's protecting wing.*
>
> —Andrew Johnson[17]

Ulysses S. Grant

#18

1869–1877

Republican

Born: April 27, 1822

Died: July 23, 1885

1869–1870

- ☆ Ulysses S. Grant takes office
- ☆ America's first professional baseball team is formed
- ☆ The U.S. Census counts 39.8 million Americans

Illustration of the birthplace of Ulysses S. Grant

Ulysses S. Grant was born in 1822 in Ohio. When he was 17, he entered the U.S. Military Academy at West Point and developed a reputation as a fearless horseman. After graduating, Grant served under General Zachary Taylor during the Mexican-American War where he learned a lot about warfare.

Union Brigadier General Ulysses S. Grant, 1861

After retiring from the military in 1854, Grant struggled as a farmer and a businessman. When the Civil War began, he was appointed to train volunteers in Illinois and quickly rose through the ranks as he proved successful on the battlefield. In 1864, he achieved the rank of lieutenant general, a rank that had previously only been awarded to George Washington and Winfield Scott. In this position, he led the Union to victory over the Confederacy. After the war, he became a leading candidate for the presidency, and he chose to run for office.

The surrender of General Lee to General Grant at Appomattox Court House

Ulysses S. Grant became president when he won the elections of 1868 and 1872. In office, he devoted his time to the issue of Reconstruction. He also suppressed the Ku Klux Klan and saw passage of the 15th Amendment that gave freed slaves the right to vote. However, Northerners were unhappy with an economic depression, and white Southerners were fighting to deny African Americans their civil rights. These problems (and a few scandals) prevented President Grant from being elected to a third term.

1873–1874

☆ P. T. Barnum's "Greatest Show on Earth" opens

☆ "Boss" Tweed, a New York Democratic Party leader, is convicted of fraud

1875–1876

☆ Aristides wins the first Kentucky Derby (horse race)

☆ Alexander Graham Bell patents the telephone

President Trivia Games

Who Am I?
1974–1977
See page 82

Trivia: Who became president after John F. Kennedy was assassinated?
See page 78

In 1873, the *Virginius* incident nearly thrust the U.S. into a war with Spain. The incident began when the U.S. merchant ship *Virginius* was taken captive by a Spanish warship for illegally carrying war materials and men to insurgents in Cuba (which happened to be owned by Spain at the time). Fifty-three of the passengers and crew of the *Virginius* were executed and many Americans called for war with Spain. However, after Spain's president apologized for the tragedy and paid a cash settlement to the families of the executed Americans, war was avoided. The U.S. government did not authorize the shipment of war materials.

Alexander Graham Bell at the opening of the long-distance line from New York to Chicago in 1892

Many inventions were developed during Grant's time as president including the phone. Alexander Graham Bell patented the telephone in 1876. Ironically, he believed the invention to be an intrusion on his scientific work and refused to have one in his study.

The Cincinnati Red Stockings hit the fields in 1869 as America's first professional baseball team. The Red Stockings defeated all its opponents, finishing the season with a 57–0 record. It is said that Grant's carriage stopped for several moments to watch part of a game.

A lithograph of the 1869 Cincinnati Red Stockings' baseball player

> *Although a soldier by profession,*
> *I have never felt any sort of fondness for war,*
> *and I have never advocated it,*
> *except as a means of peace.*
>
> —Ulysses S. Grant[18]

Rutherford B. Hayes

#19

1877–1881

Republican

Born: October 4, 1822

Died: January 17, 1893

1877–1878

- ☆ Rutherford B. Hayes takes office
- ☆ Thomas Edison invents the phonograph
- ☆ Electricity is furnished to some homes

Rutherford B. Hayes was born in Ohio in 1822. His father died shortly before his birth and an uncle acted as guardian. Hayes received a quality education and graduated from Harvard Law School in 1845. He began practicing law in his home state and, in 1852, married Lucy Webb. When the Civil War began, he quickly joined the Union forces.

Rutherford B. Hayes and his wife, Lucy, on their wedding day, Dec. 30, 1852

During the war, Hayes rose to the rank of brigadier general and became popular. After the war, he became a U.S. representative and, a few years later, Ohio's governor. Then, with the 1876 presidential election approaching, he found himself the Republican nominee for president. However, because of scandals in the Grant administration (yes, Grant was a Republican too), the old commander was facing another tough battle that many thought he would lose.

Rutherford B. Hayes in Civil War uniform in 1861

When the ballots were counted in the 1876 presidential election, Democrat Samuel Tilden received nearly 250,000 more votes than Rutherford B. Hayes, but Hayes became president anyway. How so? Because Hayes won the most electoral votes!

1876 U.S. presidential candidate Samuel Jones Tilden

1879

- ☆ Thomas Edison perfects the light bulb

- ☆ Knights of Labor go public, hoping to help the working class

1880

- ☆ France begins work on the Panama Canal in Central America
- ☆ The U.S. Census counts 50.1 million Americans

- ☆ Cha-ching, the first cash register is patented

President Trivia Games

Who Am I?
1881–1885
See page 48

Trivia: Who was president when the Oklahoma Land Rush began?
See page 52

President Hayes and his cabinet

In office, President Hayes withdrew federal troops from reconstructive states. Sadly, this left the door wide open in the South for the segregation of whites and blacks to enter and civil rights to exit. When it came time for the next election, President Hayes decided not to run. Jim Crow Laws spread through the South when President Hayes was in office and had lasting effects.

Campaign banner for the 1876 Republican presidential ticket

> *What a great mistake the man makes who goes about to oppose this religion! What a crime, if we may judge of men's acts by their results! Nay, what a great mistake is made by him who does not support the religion of the Bible!*
>
> —Rutherford B. Hayes[19]

James A. Garfield

1881–1881

Republican

Born: November 19, 1831

Died: September 19, 1881

#20

1881

☆ James A. Garfield takes office

☆ Frederick Douglass is appointed recorder of deeds for Washington, D.C.

President James Garfield birthplace, with a log cabin replica, Moreland Hills, Ohio

When the Civil War started, Garfield volunteered to fight, joining the Union side. He was first given the task of securing Kentucky. He was successful with this assignment and soon rose through the ranks. Garfield won one of the most important minor battles of the Civil War when he defeated Confederate General Humphery Marshall in eastern Kentucky. With only 1,100 men, Garfield pushed the Confederate force of 5,000 out of the state.

James A. Garfield was born in a log cabin in Ohio in 1831. He was raised in what was then known as "The Wilderness." In 1854, he graduated from Williams College with the highest honors in his class and went on to become a college president, a state senator, and a major general in the U.S. Army.

Grand national Republican banner for 1880

General James Garfield

After the war, Garfield returned to Ohio where he entered politics and, as he had done on the field of battle, rose through the ranks. As the 1880 presidential election approached, he decided to run for the nation's highest office, the presidency. James A. Garfield won the election of 1880 and took the oath of office on March 4, 1881. He stated in his inaugural address that it was important for African Americans to be treated as full citizens and that illiteracy was a huge problem in America. Tragically, on July 2 of that year, while President Garfield was walking through a train station, he was

1881

☆ Clara Barton founds the American Red Cross

☆ President Garfield is shot twice

1881

☆ Booker T. Washington helps establish the Tuskegee Institute

☆ Ailing President Garfield is moved to Jersey Shore

☆ President Garfield dies

President Trivia Games

Who Am I?
1825–1829
See page 18

Trivia: Who caught a cold and died shortly after becoming president?
See page 24

shot twice by a man who was upset for not getting a government job. The wounded president was unable to make a full recovery and died a few months later.

James A. Garfield's assassination

The Tuskegee Institute (now known as Tuskegee University) was founded in Tuskegee, Alabama, in 1881, just after Garfield was shot. With the help of Booker T. Washington, the school became a pillar of education for many African Americans who were being discriminated against because of the color of their skin.

Garfield Monument, Golden Gate Park, San Francisco, California

Clara Barton was a humanitarian who helped Civil War soldiers as early as 1861. After the war, she visited Europe and was introduced to the Red Cross organization. She later returned to the States and, in 1881, established the American Red Cross. President Garfield recognized the organization for its powerful influence. For over a century the American Red Cross has been helping millions of people during times of war and natural disasters. It is best known for conducting blood drives and for providing food and medical attention to those in need.

> *If wrinkles must be written on our brows,*
> *let them not be written upon the heart.*
> *The spirit should never grow old.*
>
> —James A. Garfield[20]

Chester A. Arthur

#21

1881–1885

Republican

Born: October 5, 1829

Died: November 18, 1886

1881

- ☆ Chester A. Arthur takes office
- ☆ The shootout at the OK Corral occurs in Arizona where Wyatt Earp is a lawman

Chester A. Arthur was born in Vermont in 1829. He attended prep schools and later graduated with a degree from Union College in New York. Afterward, he became a teacher and then a successful lawyer. In New York City, he helped end segregation of the city's transit systems.

Following the death of President Garfield, Judge Brady administering the presidential oath to Vice President Arthur

During the Civil War, Arthur held high posts in the New York militia. He returned to his law practice after the war and then became Collector of the Port of New York, a very powerful position at that time. When it came time for the 1880 presidential election, the Republican Party chose James A. Garfield as its presidential candidate and Arthur as its vice-presidential candidate. The two men won the election and Arthur became the nation's newest vice president.

Chester A. Arthur became president after President Garfield passed away from a gunshot wound, and in a short period, nearly all of Garfield's cabinet members resigned. Only Todd Lincoln, son of President Lincoln, remained. One of Arthur's greatest achievements was getting a law passed that made people take written examinations to prove they were worthy of certain government jobs. But despite that, he couldn't secure the Republican Party's nomination in the next presidential election and retired from politics.

Chester A. Arthur statue at Madison Square in New York City

1882–1883

- ☆ The electric iron is patented
- ☆ The Hatfield-McCoy feud begins in the Appalachian Mountains
- ☆ "Buffalo Bill" Cody performs his first Wild West Show

1884

- ☆ Alaska becomes a U.S. Territory
- ☆ An African American is elected chairman of the Republican Convention

President Trivia Games

Who Am I?
1929–1933
See page 68

Trivia: Who became president after Theodore Roosevelt left office?
See page 60

The Hatfield Clan in 1897

The Hatfield-McCoy Feud began when President Arthur was in office. The Hatfield clan (mostly from West Virginia) and the McCoy clan (mostly from Kentucky) didn't like each other for a host of reasons. They were predominantly on opposite sides during the Civil War (the Hatfields favored the Confederacy and the McCoys favored the Union), and they had a few encounters in court. On August 7, 1882, feelings between the two families took a turn for the worse when members of both families showed up at a Kentucky voting site during an election. Words were traded and then knives and gunshots. Ellison Hatfield died after being stabbed 26 times and shot. Following his death, the three McCoys that were believed to have been responsible were seized, tied to bushes, and shot to death by members of the Hatfield family. The feud was on.

The Hatfield-McCoy Feud led to the deaths of more than a dozen members of the two families and gained national attention. The governors of West Virginia and Kentucky were compelled to call up their state militias to restore order, and West Virginia's governor once threatened to have his militia invade Kentucky! The feud ended in 1891 when the families agreed to stop fighting each other.

> *The extravagant expenditure of public money is an evil not to be measured by the value of that people who are taxed for it.*
>
> —Chester A. Arthur[21]

Grover Cleveland

1885–1889

Democrat

Born: March 18, 1837

Died: June 24, 1908

#22

1885–1886

- ☆ Grover Cleveland takes office
- ☆ The Statue of Liberty (a gift from France) arrives in New York
- ☆ Chief Geronimo surrenders to the U.S.
- ☆ Anti-Chinese violence escalates in Seattle

Caldwell Presbyterian parsonage, birthplace of Grover Cleveland

Grover Cleveland was born in 1837 in Caldwell, New Jersey, and later moved with his family to New York where he spent much of his childhood. After his father died, Cleveland supported his family by becoming a teacher. Later, he moved to Buffalo and worked for his uncle. Here, he met influential men, studied hard, and became a lawyer.

During the Civil War, Cleveland continued to practice law and support his mother and younger sisters. He was elected sheriff of New York's Erie County when he was only 33 years old and personally carried out the executions of several men. Afterward, his popularity grew. He became mayor of Buffalo and then New York's governor.

Grover Cleveland's first cabinet, 1885

When it came time for the 1884 presidential election, Cleveland threw his hat into the ring and secured the Democratic Party's nomination.

Grover Cleveland won the election of 1884 and took the oath of office in 1885. As president, he worked to reform the federal government. He created the Interstate Commerce Commission; modernized the navy; and, for the most part, hired people to government positions based upon their merit and not based upon their party loyalties.

Frances Folsom Cleveland

The United States received the Statue of Liberty from France during President Cleveland's first term. The gift (located on Liberty Island in New York Harbor) was dedicated on October 28, 1886, and is a robed female figure that represents Libertas, the Roman symbol of freedom. Initially,

1887

☆ Helen Keller learns "water" from her teacher

☆ Mighty Casey strikes out against the New York Giants

1888–1889

☆ Frederick Douglass is nominated for president

☆ Washington Monument completed

President Trivia Games

Who Am I?
1841–1841
See page 24

Trivia: Who became president after Richard Nixon resigned?
See page 82

the statue was intended to serve as a lighthouse, but the light of the torch was too dim to be useful. Also, when it was built, the statue had a dull copper color. However, shortly after 1900, a green patina (caused by oxidation of the statue's covering) grew over the statue's surface, giving it its current green appearance. Still, despite its change of color, the Statue of Liberty remains unchanged as a symbol of freedom, especially to the many boatloads of immigrants that saw the towering figure when they entered the U.S. through New York Harbor.

Unveiling of the Statue of Liberty Enlightening the World (1886) by Edward Moran

During President Cleveland's second year in office, he married 21 year-old Frances Folsom, the youngest First Lady ever! However, her stay in the White House was short-lived because, in the next election, President Cleveland got the most popular votes but not the most electoral votes.

1888 Democratic nominees for president

After President Cleveland's defeat in the election of 1888, First Lady Frances Cleveland told the White House staff that she would be returning in four years. As history would show, she was correct.

> *I know as no one else can know my limitations, and how fixed and inexorable they are . . . but I shall trust God, as I have in the past, for strength and opportunity for further usefulness.*
>
> —Grover Cleveland[22]

Benjamin Harrison

#23

1889–1893

Republican

Born: August 20, 1833

Died: March 13, 1901

1889–1890

- ☆ Benjamin Harrison takes office
- ☆ White settlers begin moving into the Oklahoma Territory
- ☆ Wyoming becomes the first state to give women the right to vote

Benjamin Harrison was born in Ohio in 1833. He was the grandson of President William Henry Harrison and the second of nine children. After graduating from college, he began studying law. He married Caroline Scott in 1853 and, a year later, began practicing law in Indiana.

During the Civil War, Harrison felt the need to join the Union Army. He signed up, served with William T. Sherman, and climbed to the rank of brigadier general. After the war, he returned to Indiana where he became a U.S. senator. A few years later, in 1888, he became the Republican Party's surprise nominee for president.

Brigadier General Harrison (left) with other commanders, 1865

In the election of 1888, Benjamin Harrison defeated incumbent President Grover Cleveland to become America's newest president. This election was one of the rare occasions where the winner actually received fewer popular votes than his opponent.

Harrison-Morton campaign poster

As president, Harrison raised tariffs, gave pensions to disabled Civil War veterans, and passed the first federal law to curb powerful monopolies. The American frontier was expanding as well.

The Oklahoma Land Rush began at high noon on April 22, 1889. At that time, approximately 50,000 people rushed into areas of Oklahoma that were originally Indian Territory to stake their claims to the land. Still, some people broke the law by entering the open territory early and hiding. Then, when the legal time of entry had passed, these individuals (called "Sooners") came

Inauguration of Benjamin Harrison

1891

☆ American Express issues its first traveler's checks

☆ The game of basketball is created in Massachusetts

1892–1893

☆ The General Electric Company is formed

☆ Hawaii becomes a republic after deposing its queen

President Trivia Games

Who Am I?

1845–1849

See page 28

Trivia: Which president died after being shot in a train station?

See page 46

out of hiding and staked their claims on prime land. Over time, more and more settlers moved to Oklahoma, thus paving the way for Oklahoma becoming a state in 1907.

Years before the 1889 Oklahoma Land Rush, all of Oklahoma was Indian Territory and off limits to U.S. settlement. However, the U.S. government forced the Indians residing in Oklahoma to sign new treaties that shrank the Indian Territory. The Oklahoma land that the Indians gave up became the new property of the U.S. government, and the government, in turn, opened a large chunk of the newly acquired land for development to predominantly white settlers.

The Indian tribes living in Oklahoma at the time of the Land Rush were originally from areas east of the Mississippi River. These tribes (which included the Creek, Choctaw, Cherokee, Chickasaw, and Seminole nations) were relocated during the 1830s because they didn't want to assimilate and become American citizens.

Harrison's Cabinet with him in the lower right

In 1892, President Harrison lost his re-election bid to the same man he defeated in 1888 (President Grover Cleveland). He returned to his law practice after leaving office.

> *We Americans have no commission from God to police the world.*
>
> —Benjamin Harrison[23]

The Oklahoma Land Rush

Grover Cleveland

#24

1893–1897

Democrat

Born: March 18, 1837

Died: June 24, 1908

1893

☆ Grover Cleveland takes office

☆ The Panic of 1893 triggers bank failures

☆ Many Chinese people are deported from San Francisco

Remember this guy? It's Grover Cleveland again, both the 22nd and 24th President of the United States. If you don't remember much about his early life you can turn a few pages back and read all about it. Oh, and one more thing that wasn't mentioned before: Grover Cleveland is a comeback kid!

Grover Cleveland's last cabinet

After being defeated by Harrison in the 1888 presidential election, Cleveland and his wife moved to New York City. Cleveland joined a law firm and saw the birth of his first child, Ruth. He also wrote an open letter dealing with politics that boosted his popularity. When it was time for another presidential election, the Democratic Party decided to back Cleveland again.

The election of 1892 featured the same two candidates from the previous election (Grover Cleveland and Benjamin Harrison), but the outcome was different. This time, Cleveland was the winner.

Jacob Coxey at the U.S. Capitol in 1914

After taking office for his second time, President Cleveland was faced with the Panic of 1893 and what was to become a six-year economic depression. The crisis was worse than any American had ever seen before. Nearly 20 percent of the workforce was left without work, and many Americans who couldn't meet their mortgage payments simply walked away from their homes.

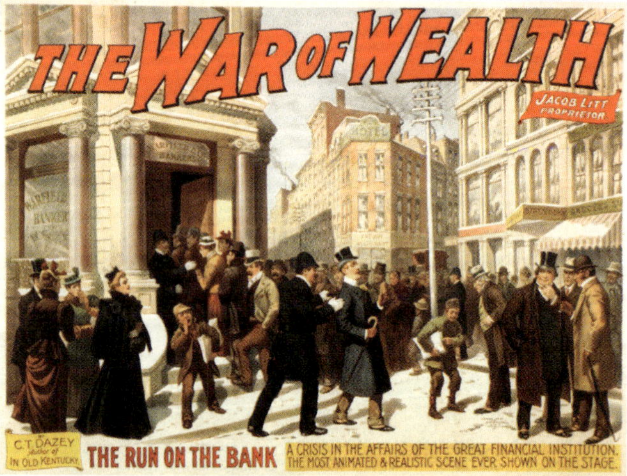

The 1896 Broadway melodrama *The War of Wealth* was inspired by the Panic of 1893.

1894

- ☆ Over 130,000 miners in Ohio go on strike for pay increases
- ☆ The American Railway Union goes on strike

1895–1896

- ☆ The game of volleyball is invented in Massachusetts
- ☆ A moving picture projector is patented
- ☆ The X-ray machine is demonstrated in the U.S.

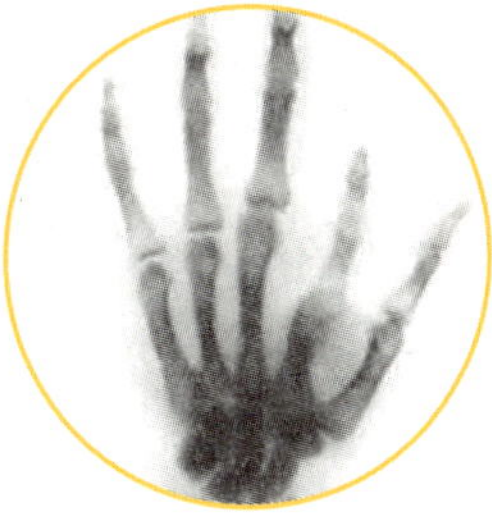

Did You Know?

Trivia: What is the term limit of a United States president?

Answer: Two four-year terms

In 1894, "Coxey's Army" marched to Washington, D.C., to oppose the federal government's handling of the depression. The "army" was composed mostly of unemployed workers, led by Jacob Coxey, and numbered about 100 men when it first began its journey from Massillon, Ohio. Nearly a month later, the protesters reached the capital and their numbers swelled to nearly 6,000 people. Coxey and other leaders were arrested for walking on the grass of the U.S. Capitol and the protest came to a quick halt.

In winning the election of 1892, President Cleveland set himself apart from all U.S. presidents (both before and after) by becoming the only president to leave office and later return.

When it came time for the next election, President Cleveland declined his party's nomination and retired.

The pro-Republican *Judge* magazine blamed the Panic of 1893 on the Democratic victory in the 1892 election.

> *Public officers are the servants and agents of the people, to execute the laws which the people have made.*
>
> —Grover Cleveland[24]

William McKinley

#25

1897–1901

Republican

Born: January 29, 1843

Died: September 14, 1901

1897

☆ William McKinley takes office

☆ Nineteen striking miners are killed by police in Lattimer, PA

First Lady of the U.S. Ida Saxton McKinley

William McKinley was born in Ohio in 1843. He fought with the Union Army during the Civil War and obtained the rank of captain. After the war, he became a lawyer and opened a law practice in Canton, Ohio. McKinley married Ida Saxon in 1871. They had two daughters that died before seeing the age of five.

William and Ida McKinley pose in front of the McKinley home.

McKinley also served as a prosecuting attorney in Ohio and became active in politics when he campaigned for his old commander, Rutherford B. Hayes, who was running for Ohio's governor at the time. In turn, Hayes helped McKinley get elected to the U.S. House of Representatives. A few years later, McKinley was elected Ohio's governor and, when his term was finished, set his sights on the White House.

1900 re-election poster with the theme that McKinley has returned prosperity to America

1898

- ☆ The USS *Maine* explodes and sinks in Cuba
- ☆ The Spanish-American War begins
- ☆ The machine gun is first used in battle

1899–1901

- ☆ The Spanish-American War ends
- ☆ The U.S. Census counts 76.2 million Americans
- ☆ President McKinley is assassinated

President Trivia Games

Who Am I?
2017–2021
See page 96

Trivia: Who picked a woman to be his vice president?
See page 98

William McKinley became president by winning the election of 1896. In office, he led the U.S. to victory in the Spanish-American War. He also pushed to make American producers more valuable in the world. On the home front, President McKinley supported civil rights to all African Americans, but he was unwilling to use federal power to stop many injustices that were taking place in the nation. He was re-elected to a second term in 1900 and was assassinated less than a year later. It was after this that Congress requested that presidents be protected by the Secret Service.

Starboard bow view of USS *Maine*

The unexplained explosion of the USS *Maine* in Havana Harbor in 1898 was one spark that led to the Spanish-American War. Many Americans believed Spain was responsible for sinking the ship.

A 1900 Republican campaign poster for the U.S. presidential election

> *War should never be entered upon until every agency of peace has failed.*
>
> —William McKinley[25]

Theodore Roosevelt

1901–1909

Republican

Born: October 27, 1858

Died: January 6, 1919

#26

1901–1904

- ☆ Theodore Roosevelt takes office
- ☆ The U.S. takes over construction of the Panama Canal
- ☆ The Wright brothers fly the first successful airplane
- ☆ The U.S. ends its occupation of Cuba

Colonel Roosevelt and the Rough Riders after capturing Kettle Hill

Theodore Roosevelt was born in 1858 in New York. As a child, he was asthmatic and often had to sleep either propped up in bed or slouching in a chair. At the age of seven, he developed a love for zoology (the study of animals) that stayed with him the rest of his life. He also took boxing lessons to combat his poor physical condition.

Colonel Theodore Roosevelt

After graduating from Harvard College in 1880, Roosevelt underwent a physical examination and was instructed by his doctor to avoid strenuous activity due to serious heart problems. However, instead of finding a desk job, Roosevelt stayed on the move. He joined the U.S. Army and became a war hero riding with the calvary in the Spanish-American War. Shortly after leaving the army, he was elected New York's governor. He then became President McKinley's vice president.

Roosevelt family at Oyster Bay, c. 1903

After President McKinley was killed, Theodore Roosevelt became president and a popular one at that. After completing McKinley's term, President Roosevelt was elected to two more and then retired. In office, he worked to curb the power of large corporations; passed legislation to ban misleading advertising; and began holding press briefings with reporters, something that was never done before. Four years after retiring, he came back and ran for the presidency again! This

1907–1908

☆ Automatic washers and dryers are available to public

☆ The Gideon Bible is placed in its first hotel room

☆ Henry Ford introduces the Model T automobile

1909

☆ The first U.S. fleet to circle the globe returns to port

☆ U.S. penny is changed to one with Abraham Lincoln

President Trivia Games

Who Am I?
1989–1993
See page 88

Trivia: Who was president during the 9/11 terrorist attacks?
See page 92

First flight of the Wright Flyer, Orville piloting, Wilbur running at wingtip

time, he ran under the new "Bull Moose" Party. Roosevelt lost this election and went back into retirement.

A 1902 political cartoon in *The Washington Post* spawned the teddy bear name.

In 1902, the U.S. took over the construction of the Panama Canal after the French abandoned the project because of high costs and having incurred over 20,000 deaths, mostly due to disease. When the canal was completed in 1914, the waterway created a vital link between the Atlantic and Pacific Oceans.

Yes, the "teddy bear" gets its name from President Theodore Roosevelt. After learning the president refused to shoot a tied-up bear, Morris Michtom began making stuffed bear cub toys. He labeled them as "Teddy's bear" to help sales, and the rest is history.

On December 17, 1903, Orville and Wilbur Wright flew into history when their airplane successfully took to the air in North Carolina. The brothers were from Ohio, but they selected North Carolina as the place for their flight because of the favorable wind conditions there. The flight only lasted 12 seconds, but it was enough to propel the world into a new age! In 1910, Roosevelt became the first president to take a flight in a plane.

> *Church work and church attendance mean the cultivation of the habit of feeling some responsibility for others.*
>
> —Theodore Roosevelt[26]

William H. Taft

1909–1913

Republican

Born: September 15, 1857

Died: March 8, 1930

#27

1909–1910

☆ William H. Taft takes office

☆ The U.S. Census counts 92.2 million Americans

☆ Earth passes through the tail of Halley's Comet

William Howard Taft inauguration

William Taft was born in Ohio in 1857. He graduated from both Yale College and the Cincinnati Law School. He then began a legal career, which helped him to become a judge to the Ohio Superior Court, the U.S. solicitor general, and a judge on the U.S. Court of Appeals.

Taft also served as the governor-general of the Philippines from 1901 to 1903. He was later offered a seat on the Supreme Court, a position he aspired to attain, but he turned it down to help the Philippines reach the capacity to govern itself. A year later, in 1904, he became President Roosevelt's secretary of war. When President Roosevelt decided not to run for the presidency in 1908, Taft became the Republican Party's choice.

McKinley-Theodore Roosevelt-William H. Taft Postcard, 1908

1908 Republican candidates

With the backing of President Roosevelt, William H. Taft easily won the election of 1908 and became America's newest president. In office, he created a postal service system for delivering mail within the states and supported a federal income tax. When the next election came around, he and Roosevelt (who decided that he wanted to be president again) wrestled for control of the Republican Party. Taft was able to secure the

1911

☆ Let's cook! Crisco® shortening hits the stores

☆ First Indianapolis 500 is run

1912–1913

☆ The *Titanic* sinks in the Atlantic Ocean

☆ Theodore Roosevelt starts the "Bull Moose" Party

☆ Federal income tax is once again the law of the land

President Trivia Games

Who Am I?
1841–1845
See page 26

Trivia: Who became president after Warren G. Harding died in 1923?
See page 66

Republican Party's nomination, which prompted Roosevelt to march off and start his own political party, the "Bull Moose" Party. Both men ended up losing the election of 1912 to Woodrow Wilson, a Democrat.

RMS *Titanic* departing Southampton on April 10, 1912

In 1910, Halley's Comet made its usual 75- to 76-year appearance in our solar system and (with the help of expansive newspaper coverage) fueled fear in many that the end of the world might be near. What didn't help matters was the fact the comet passed so close that the earth actually passed through the comet's 24-million-mile-long tail for six hours! Telescope sales were astronomical, President Taft made a visit to the U.S. Naval Observatory to get a closer look, and hotels in large cities were filled with people wanting to get to their high rooftops to see the rare visitor. After the earth passed through the comet's tail, many people breathed a sigh of relief and went back to their normal business. The planet wasn't doomed after all.

American author Samuel Clemens (also known as Mark Twain) was born when Halley's Comet visited our solar system in 1835. In 1909, just one year prior to the comet's return, he said, "I came in with Halley's Comet in 1835. It is coming again next year, and I expect to go out with it."[27] His expectations were correct. Shortly after the comet reached perihelion, Mark Twain died.

The RMS *Titanic* hit an iceberg and sank in the Atlantic Ocean in April of 1912 — 1,517 people died in frigid waters. A dear friend of Taft's died in the disaster, and he openly wept over his loss.

Halley's comet

> *I love judges, and I love courts. They are my ideals, that typify on earth what we shall meet hereafter in heaven under a just God.*
>
> —William H. Taft[28]

Woodrow Wilson

#28

1913–1921

Democrat

Born: December 28, 1856

Died: February 3, 1924

1913–1914

- ☆ Woodrow Wilson takes office
- ☆ The Panama Canal opens
- ☆ World War I begins in Europe

Woodrow Wilson's boyhood home in Augusta, Georgia

Woodrow Wilson was born in Virginia in 1856. He didn't learn to read until he was over ten years old, probably due to dyslexia. Wilson learned shorthand to compensate for his reading deficiency and went on to become a lawyer. In 1883, he left his law practice to study history and political science to prep himself for a career in politics.

Wilson giving his first State of the Union address

Between 1883 and 1902, Wilson wrote and spoke about what he saw as flaws in America's political system. He then became president of Princeton University and, in 1910, the governor of New Jersey. As governor, he introduced worker's compensation and revamped many political processes. With support for him growing, Wilson decided to make a run for the nation's highest office. He became the Democratic Party's nominee in 1912.

Wilson accepting the Democratic Party nomination, 1916

Woodrow Wilson won the election of 1912 and, four years later, the election of 1916. As president, he became a leader in the Progressive Era, a period of reform. In office, he worked with Congress to pass the 18th Amendment (which prohibited the sale of alcoholic beverages) and the 19th Amendment (which gave women the right to vote). He also led America through World War I. President Wilson suffered a stroke that left him in a wheelchair for a while and didn't seek a third term due to his declining health.

1917–1919

- ☆ Russia's Communist Revolution begins
- ☆ World War I ends
- ☆ First Red Scare in U.S., with fear of anarchism in Russia

1920

- ☆ The League of Nations is created, but the U.S. doesn't join
- ☆ The U.S. Census counts 106 million Americans
- ☆ The 19th Amendment gives women the right to vote

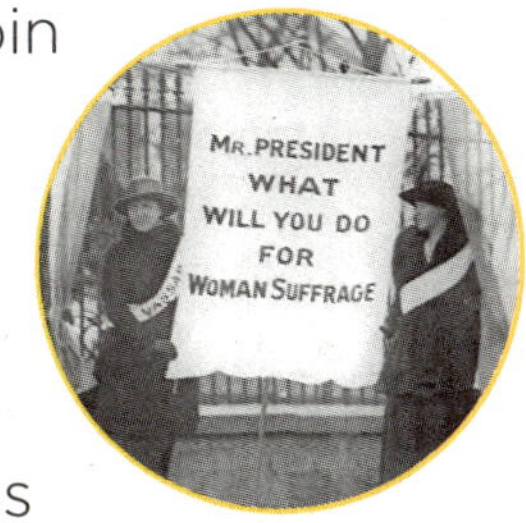

President Trivia Games

Who Am I?

1817–1825

See page 16

Trivia: Which president served two non-consecutive terms?

See pages 50, 54

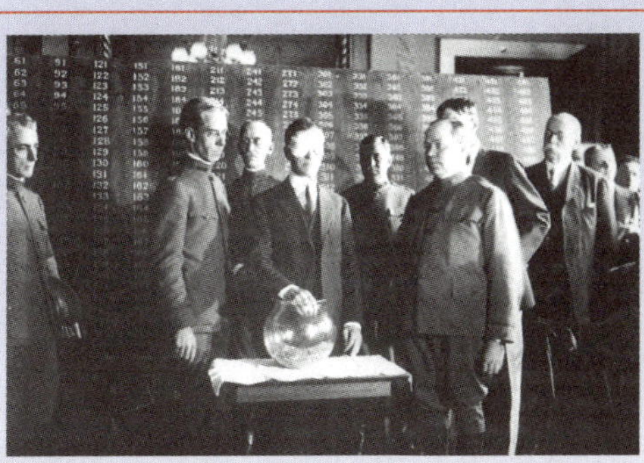

Secretary of War Newton Baker drawing the first draft number of those to serve in the American forces during World War I

During World War I, President Wilson passed laws that suppressed America's freedom of speech. Many citizens were imprisoned for saying they disagreed with America's involvement in the war and others were even jailed for criticizing the Red Cross and YMCA!

The United States entered World War I during the third year of the conflict in 1917. Joining the Allied Powers of France, the British Empire, Russia, Italy, and various other smaller nations, American soldiers traveled to Europe to fight against the Central Powers of Germany, Austria-Hungry, the Ottoman Empire, and Bulgaria. The introduction of U.S. soldiers helped break a stalemate in the trenches of France and ultimately led to an Allied victory. In the war's aftermath, the German people had to make restitutions for war damages that led to hyperinflation, a hungry German populous, and the eventual rise of Adolf Hitler, who promised a better and stronger Germany. Many thought World War I would be the "war to end all wars," but they were wrong. Though the U.S. helped stop the fighting in 1918, the seeds for World War II were sown.

Nearly 120,000 American soldiers died during the short time that the U.S. fought during World War I, and another 200,000 were wounded.

Men of U.S. 64th Regiment, 7th Infantry Division, celebrating the news of the Armistice

> *Liberty has never come from Government. Liberty has always come from the subjects of it. The history of liberty is the history of limitations of governmental power, not the increase of it.*
>
> —Woodrow Wilson[29]

Warren G. Harding

#29

1921–1923

Republican

Born: November 2, 1865

Died: August 2, 1923

1921

- ☆ Warren G. Harding takes office
- ☆ Congress approves the construction of the Tomb of the Unknown Soldier
- ☆ The Chicago "Black Sox" baseball scandal goes to court

President Harding and Presidential Party in Alaska on Presidential Train

Warren Harding was born in 1865 in Ohio. After college, he and some friends bought a newspaper in Marion, Ohio, and went to work. Harding became very exhausted in his new business and spent time recovering in a sanitarium. A few years later, he married Florence DeWolfe.

With his newspaper and his wife supporting him, Harding was elected to the Ohio State Senate. He later became Ohio's lieutenant governor and lost in his attempt to become governor. After this setback, he bounced back and became a U.S. Senator. He served in this position for several years and became the Republican Party's choice for president in 1920.

During the campaign, he promised "a return to normalcy," which meant, in part, that he didn't want America involved in international affairs, especially if it meant war. In office, he established what became known as the Department of Veterans Affairs to help war veterans in need, and he helped lead America out of an economic depression.

During the campaign, Harding took advantage of the public's growing hostility toward Woodrow Wilson, the Democratic president. Many Americans didn't want the U.S. to join the Wilson-sponsored League of Nations, the U.S. economy was in a recession, and large groups of Americans of European descent were outraged at Wilson's wartime policies. As a result, the Republicans won the election, with Harding capturing 404 electoral votes (60% of the popular vote) and Cox gathering only 127 electoral votes (34% of the popular vote). Tragically, Harding died of a heart attack about midway through his term.

The 1919 Chicago White Sox became known as the Chicago "Black Sox" because some of its players took money to lose the World Series. In 1921, the accused players had to answer to charges in a highly publicized court trial. Harding was a baseball fan and actually met several times with Babe Ruth.

After the Nineteenth Amendment to the U.S. Constitution was ratified in August of 1920, the

1919 Chicago White Sox

1922

- ☆ Many new American radio stations hit the airwaves

- ☆ The U.S. launches its first aircraft carrier
- ☆ King Tut's tomb is discovered in Egypt

1923

- ☆ *Time Magazine* hits the newsstands
- ☆ President Harding dies

President Trivia Games

Who Am I?
1789–1797
See page 8

Trivia: Who became president after James Garfield was assassinated?
See page 48

President Warren G. Harding's first cabinet meeting

presidential election of 1920 became unique because, for the first time in American history, women nationwide were given the right to vote! The leading candidates during this election were Warren G. Harding (Republican) and James M. Cox (Democrat).

President Harding commuted the jail sentence of American socialist Eugene Debs, effective Christmas Day, 1921. Debs was a union leader who was openly opposed to U.S. involvement in World War I when Woodrow Wilson was president. He was arrested in 1918 and imprisoned for sedition in 1919. President Wilson said that Debs was a "traitor to this country" for speaking out against American involvement in the war, but President Harding perceived the ten-year sentence as being too harsh and let Debs go free.

Harding Memorial in Marion, Ohio

In addition to being a union leader, Eugene Debs was also active in politics. He ran for president as a socialist in 1900, 1904, 1908, and 1920. He received more and more votes with each election but never more than 6 percent of the total cast. He was still in jail during his 1920 run!

> *It is my conviction that the fundamental trouble with the people of the United States is that they have gotten too far away from Almighty God.*
>
> —Warren G. Harding[30]

Calvin Coolidge

1923–1929

Republican

Born: July 4, 1872

Died: January 5, 1933

#30

1923–1924

- ☆ Calvin Coolidge takes office
- ☆ Edwin Hubble announces existence of other galaxies

Calvin Coolidge with his family

Calvin Coolidge was born on July 4 (Independence Day), 1872, in Vermont. When he was 12, his mother died. In 1898, Coolidge opened a law office in Massachusetts and gained a reputation as a diligent attorney. As a result, many local businesses utilized his services. Coolidge then became active in politics and married.

Coolidge served the city of Northampton in a number of positions before winning a seat to the Massachusetts House of Representatives. Here, he was known as a progressive Republican, supporting women's rights to vote and the direct election of U.S. senators who, at the time, were elected by state legislatures. He eventually climbed the political ladder and became vice president of the United States.

Calvin Coolidge became president after President Warren G. Harding died then went on to win the election of 1924. As president during the "Roaring Twenties," he and Congress lowered taxes to the point where over 95 percent of all Americans didn't pay an income tax! His popularity, however, sagged due to his slow response in sending federal aid to help those affected by the Great Mississippi Flood of 1927, which led to the deaths of over 200 people and caused over $400 million in damages.

President Coolidge signed the Immigration Act of 1924. This federal law limited the number of immigrants who could be admitted into the U.S. to no more than 2 percent of people from that country who were already living in America as of 1890. However, one discriminatory aspect of the law forbade immigration from the "undesirable" Asian-Pacific Triangle countries (Japan, China,

A "tent-city" in Vicksburg following the Great Mississippi Flood of 1927

1925–1926

- ☆ Tennessee outlaws the teaching of evolution in schools
- ☆ The Ku Klux Klan marches in Washington, D.C.
- ☆ "Talking" movies premiere in U.S. theaters

1927–1928

- ☆ Walt Disney's Mickey Mouse debuts for the first time
- ☆ A hurricane kills at least 2,500 in Florida

President Trivia Games

Who Am I?
2021–present
See page 98

Trivia: Which president recognized Jerusalem as Israel's capital?
See page 96

and other Southeast Asian nations). The new law also set no limits on immigration from Latin American countries.

The electoral map from the 1924 presidential election gave the appearance of a division between southern states and the rest of the Union. Republican Calvin Coolidge carried most northern states and all the western states. Democrat John W. Davis carried Oklahoma and the 11 southern states that fought for the Confederacy during the Civil War. Robert La Follette ran as the Progressive Party's candidate and carried Wisconsin.

Aviation showed its advancement during President Coolidge's last term in office when Charles Lindbergh, a 25-year-old U.S. Air Mail pilot, became the first person to make a solo nonstop flight from New York to Paris in an airplane. For his efforts, he won the Orteig Prize of $25,000 and a place in history. His flight was made in 1927.

Charles Lindbergh in front of his plane, *Spirit of St. Louis*

Calvin Coolidge with his vice president, Charles G. Dawes

President Coolidge didn't seek the presidency in 1928 and retired when his final term ended.

> *Men do not make laws. They do but discover them. Laws must be justified by something more than the will of the majority. They must rest on the eternal foundation of righteousness.*
>
> —Calvin Coolidge[31]

Herbert Hoover

1929–1933

Republican

Born: August 10, 1874

Died: October 20, 1964

#31

1929

- ☆ Herbert Hoover takes office
- ☆ The U.S. introduces smaller-sized currency
- ☆ The Stock Market Crash precedes the Great Depression

Herbert Hoover's birthplace cottage in West Branch, Iowa

Herbert Hoover was born in Iowa in 1874. At the age of nine, his parents died, and he became an orphan. He was bounced among a few relatives for a short time and ended up living with an uncle. In 1891, after attending night school, Hoover was admitted to Stanford University where he graduated with a degree in geology.

Crowd gathering on Wall Street after the 1929 crash

Hoover went to work in many countries throughout the world. During World War I, he led a few hundred volunteers who helped get Americans home from Europe. He also led relief efforts to help over nine million war victims. When he returned home, he became active in the U.S. government by becoming the secretary of commerce. He became very popular when he led flood relief efforts after the Mississippi River broke its banks in 1927.

Herbert Hoover with Mrs. and President Warren G. Harding in the grandstand at a baseball game

When President Coolidge decided not to run for a second term in 1928, Herbert Hoover jumped at the chance and won. In office, he confidently stated, "We in America today are nearer to the final triumph over poverty than ever before in the history of any land."[32] Unfortunately, a few months later, the great Stock Market Crash of 1929 occurred. When it came time for the next election, almost 25 percent of Americans were out of work and President Hoover was easily defeated. In 1928, Hoover had captured 58 percent of the popular vote. Four years later, he received less than 40 percent.

1930–1931

- ☆ The U.S. Census counts 122 million Americans
- ☆ Pluto is confirmed to exist
- ☆ The "Star-Spangled Banner" becomes America's national anthem

1932

- ☆ Twenty-month-old Charles Lindbergh Jr. is kidnapped and killed
- ☆ Mobster Al Capone is convicted of tax evasion

President Trivia Games

Who Am I?
1921–1923
See page 64

Trivia: Which president was in charge of the D-Day Invasion?
See page 74

Hoover Dam was built during the Great Depression, starting construction in 1931 and finishing in 1936. It was one of the largest public works projects in the history of the country and employed some 5,000 workers. The dam is 726 feet tall and is the highest concrete arch dam in the United States. Named after the president, Hoover Dam helps contain Lake Mead, the largest reservoir in America.

Hoover Dam from across the Colorado River by Ansel Adams, 1941

U.S. President Herbert Hoover and his wife Lou Henry standing at the back of a train in Belvidere, Illinois

> *I come of Quaker stock. My ancestors were persecuted for their beliefs. Here they sought and found religious freedom. By blood and conviction I stand for religious tolerance both in act and in spirit.*
>
> —Herbert Hoover[33]

Franklin D. Roosevelt

1933–1945

Democrat

Born: January 30, 1882

Died: April 12, 1945

#32

1933–1936

- ☆ Franklin D. Roosevelt takes office
- ☆ Prohibition of alcohol comes to an end
- ☆ Olympian Jesse Owens wins four gold medals in Berlin, Germany

Franklin Delano Roosevelt was born in 1882 to one of the wealthiest families in New York State. By the time he turned 26, he had become a lawyer and a husband. Over the next few years, he served as a state senator and the secretary of the navy. Roosevelt resigned from the navy in 1920. Franklin D. Roosevelt was actually the fifth cousin of President Theodore Roosevelt.

Cox and Roosevelt in Dayton, Ohio, 1920

In 1920, Roosevelt became the Democratic Party's vice-presidential candidate for the White House. He and James Cox lost this election to Warren Harding. One year later, things got tougher for Roosevelt. He became paralyzed from the waist down due to illness. Still, despite his disability, Roosevelt went on to become New York's governor and grew in popularity. When the presidential election of 1932 came around, he was the Democratic Party's choice for president.

President Roosevelt signing Social Security Act that still provides benefits to workers today

In the midst of the Great Depression, Franklin Delano Roosevelt won the election of 1932 and enacted programs to help the economy and get people back to work. His soaring popularity then carried him to victories in the presidential elections of 1936, 1940, and 1944. That's right, Roosevelt won four elections in a row! While contending with the poor economy, he had to lead the U.S. during World War II. Sadly, shortly after his fourth term began, he died of a stroke.

USS *West Virginia* was sunk by six torpedoes and two bombs during the attack on Pearl Harbor.

1939–1941

- ☆ World War II begins with Germany's invasion of Poland
- ☆ The U.S. Census counts 132 million Americans
- ☆ The U.S. enters World War II after Japan's attack

1944–1945

- ☆ The U.S. and allies launch D-Day invasion of Western Europe
- ☆ President Roosevelt dies

President Trivia Games

Who Am I?
1993–2001
See page 90

Trivia: Who was the only president to resign from office?
See page 80

Adolf Hitler began World War II in 1939 when his German forces invaded Poland. Initially, the U.S. stayed out of the conflict, but things changed after Japan attacked the U.S. fleet at Pearl Harbor, Hawaii.

Congress quickly declared war on Japan, Italy, and Germany, and President Roosevelt helped lead America and its allies to victory.

Jesse Owens was an African American athlete who won four gold medals at the 1936 Olympic Games in Berlin, Germany. At that time, Adolf Hitler was Germany's leader, and he was using propaganda to promote his concept of Aryan racial superiority. Sadly, many Germans bought into Hitler's radical ideology based on Darwin's evolutionary thoughts.

Albert Einstein receiving from Judge Phillip Forman his certificate of American citizenship

Albert Einstein was born in Germany and fled when he realized that Adolf Hitler and the Nazi Party were planning to persecute those of Jewish heritage. He soon came to the U.S. where he became an instrumental figure in developing the atomic bomb. He also became an American citizen in 1940 and expressed his appreciation for this country by saying of it, "No one humbles himself before another person or class."

President Franklin D. Roosevelt signing the Declaration of War against Japan, December 8, 1941

> *Yesterday, December 7th, 1941,*
> *a date which will live in infamy,*
> *the United States of America was suddenly*
> *and deliberately attacked by naval*
> *and air forces of the Empire of Japan.*
>
> —Franklin D. Roosevelt[34]

Harry S. Truman

1945–1953

Democrat

Born: May 8, 1884

Died: December 26, 1972

#33

1945

- ☆ Harry S. Truman becomes president
- ☆ The U.S. drops two atomic bombs on Japan
- ☆ World War II comes to an end
- ☆ The United Nations is created with 51 members

Harry S. Truman in France during World War I

Harry S. Truman was born in Missouri in 1884. He developed interests in reading, history, and music at a young age. After high school, he slept in "hobo camps" while working as a timekeeper for the railroad.

President Truman with First Lady Bess Truman

He left that job, became a clerk for a while, and then went to Europe to fight in World War I. The war brought out Truman's leadership abilities.

Truman returned to Missouri after the war and married Bess Wallace. Truman then worked in several government positions and became popular in his state. Finally, in 1934, he hit it big by winning a U.S. Senate seat. He worked tirelessly in this position and, in 1944, earned the confidence of the Democratic Party. Truman was selected to replace Henry Wallace as President Roosevelt's vice president.

Cloud from the atomic bomb rising over Nagasaki, Japan

Harry S. Truman became president after President Roosevelt died. The end of World War II came shortly after this, with the U.S. dropping two atomic bombs on Japan. The first was dropped on August 6, 1945, on the city of Hiroshima. The explosion and subsequent radiation from the blast killed nearly 200,000 people. Three days later, another

1948

- The first tape recorder is sold
- Truman desegregates armed forces

1950–1951

- The U.S. Census counts 150 million Americans
- America enters the three-year Korean War

- The 22nd Amendment places term limits on presidents

President Trivia Games

Who Am I?
1963–1969
See page 78

Trivia: Which president was once an actor and a radio sportscaster?
See page 86

atomic bomb was dropped on the city of Nagasaki where it was estimated that 100,000 people were killed. When the severity and power of America's new weapon was finally realized, Japan's leadership unconditionally surrendered, and the war came to a halt. To this day, the debate over whether or not the U.S. should have used such a weapon is still heard; however, in Truman's day, it was firmly believed that America would have lost nearly one million soldiers trying to conquer Japan with conventional weapons.

United Nations General Assembly hall in New York City

President Truman signing a proclamation declaring a national emergency and authorizing U.S. entry into the Korean War

After the war, he led America through the transition back into a peace-time economy, played a role in the creation of Israel, and conducted the Berlin Airlift when Russia blocked access to Western-held sections of the German city. He went on to win the election of 1948 and sent troops to fight in the Korean War. When his term was completed in 1953, he retired.

The United Nations was created in 1945 in hopes of bringing peace to the world. President Truman was the first to sign the charter. The organization is now composed of nearly all world nations and is headquartered in New York City. Though its hopes were for men to "beat their swords into plowshares," a biblical reference to peace, the United Nations hasn't been able to live up to such lofty aspirations. In 1947, the United Nations voted to divide the land of Palestine between Jews and Arabs. Shortly afterward, the new Jewish nation was attacked by an Arab alliance. The U.N. didn't step in to help, but Israel won the war anyway.

> *It is only the people of religious faith throughout the world who have the power to overcome the force of tyranny. It is in their beliefs that the path can be found to justice and freedom. Their religious concepts are the only sure foundation of the democratic ideal.*
>
> —Harry S. Truman[35]

Dwight D. Eisenhower

1953–1961

Republican

Born: October 14, 1890

Died: March 28, 1969

#34

1953–1955

- ☆ Dwight D. Eisenhower takes office
- ☆ The first U.S. shopping mall opens in Michigan
- ☆ Jonas Salk successfully tests a polio vaccine

Major General Dwight Eisenhower, 1942

Dwight D. Eisenhower was born in Texas in 1890 and moved to Kansas with his family. He graduated from the West Point military academy in 1911 and trained tank crews during World War I. After the war, he remained in the military where he studied military history and tank warfare. When the U.S. entered World War II, he was a one-star general.

During the war, Eisenhower helped plan Allied strategy in the Pacific, European, and African theaters of war. He was also put in charge of the D-Day Invasion and, after the war, the U.S. zone of conquered Germany. He later returned to America and, in 1952, retired from the military as a five-star general. In that same year, the "I Like Ike" campaign began, and he became the Republican Party's nominee for president.

President Eisenhower and Vice President Richard Nixon with King Saud of Saudi Arabia

Dwight D. Eisenhower won the election of 1952 and, four years later, the election of 1956. In office, he continued many of President Roosevelt's New Deal programs, began work on the Interstate Highway System, sent military aid to South Vietnam, and led the overthrow of Iran's government. He also went to work integrating the capital's public-school system to combat racial discrimination. After leaving office, the old general retired to a farm beside Pennsylvania's Gettysburg Battlefield.

President John F. Kennedy meeting with Eisenhower at Camp David, 1961

When Russia launched the world's first satellite into space on October 4, 1957, many Americans feared their Cold War foe had a technological advantage that, if left unchecked, would spell doom to the U.S. nation. The American people voiced these fears and President Eisenhower responded by ordering the civilian rocket

1956–1958

- ☆ Civil Rights Leader Martin Luther King Jr.'s home is bombed
- ☆ The U.S. sends its first satellite into space

1959–1960

- ☆ Fearing the worst, many homeowners build bomb shelters
- ☆ The U.S. Census counts 179 million Americans

- ☆ Francis Gary Power's U-2 spy plane is shot down by Russia

President Trivia Games

Who Am I?
1809–1817
See page 14

Trivia: Which president was assassinated in 1901?
See page 56

Artist's impression of *Sputnik 1* in orbit

and satellite project (called *Vanguard*) to move up its timetable and launch America's first satellite into space. Unfortunately, the December 6, 1957, attempt was a failure. Before a nationally televised audience, the rocket rose four feet into the air, lost thrust, settled on the launch pad, and exploded. Americans were again disappointed, but their hopes were raised when the launch of *Explorer I* on January 31, 1958, proved a success. The U.S. was now in the space race.

The Soviet Union's first satellite was named *Sputnik I*. America's first satellite was named *Explorer I*. *Explorer I* remained in orbit for more than 12 years. It crashed into the Pacific Ocean on March 19, 1970.

President Eisenhower declared racial discrimination a national security issue. Communists were using the issue as a point of attack in their propaganda. Martin Luther King Jr. was rising in his influence against racial inequality as Eisenhower's second term was ending.

> *In this way we are reaffirming the transcendence of religious faith in America's heritage and future; in this way we shall constantly strengthen those spiritual weapons which forever will be our country's most powerful resource, in peace or in war.*
>
> —Dwight D. Eisenhower[36]

John F. Kennedy

#35

1961-1963

Democrat

Born: May 29, 1917

Died: November 22, 1963

1961

☆ John F. Kennedy takes office

☆ The Bay of Pigs fiasco takes place in Cuba

☆ The Berlin Wall is constructed in Germany

☆ Alan Shepard becomes the first American to enter space

John F. Kennedy was born in 1917 in Massachusetts and graduated from Harvard College with a degree in international affairs in 1941. As tensions were pointing to World War II, he volunteered for the U.S. Army but was rejected due to back problems. However, the U.S. Navy gladly took him aboard.

President John F. Kennedy Meeting of the Executive Committee of the National Security Council

Lieutenant John F. Kennedy being awarded the Navy and Marine Corps Medal for heroism in rescuing members of the crew of the PT-109

John F. Kennedy commanded a PT boat during World War II. He received several medals for his service and obtained the rank of lieutenant. Kennedy became a hero during the war for his service aboard PT-109 (a torpedo patrol boat). After the war ended, he began his political career, which included him being elected to the U.S. House of Representatives in 1946 and the U.S. Senate in 1952. Four years later, he nearly became the Democratic Party's vice-presidential nominee; however, in 1960, he fared much better. He became his party's nominee for the nation's top prize, the presidency.

Kennedy became president by winning the 1960 election. During his term, he confronted the spread of Communism throughout the world. The most memorable moment occurred when the U.S. stopped the Soviet Union from building nuclear missile sites in Cuba. President Kennedy was also credited for helping put man on the moon and promoting civil rights.

The Cuban Missile Crisis of 1962 is believed to have been the closest the world has come to World War III. The crisis came about as the result of the U.S. learning that the Soviet Union and the Communist nation of Cuba were building nuclear missile bases in Cuba. The U.S. promptly quarantined the island of Cuba and demanded that the Soviets dismantle the bases and remove any offensive weapons there. The Soviets countered by stating that any attempts by America to quarantine international waters would be an act of aggression that would lead to a nuclear war. The world feared the worst, but the conflict ended when the Soviets agreed to withdraw and the U.S. promised not to invade Cuba. The world sighed in relief.

1962

☆ The Cuban Missile Crisis unfolds

☆ The U.S. and Russia escalate nuclear weapons testing

1963

☆ Martin Luther King Jr. makes his "I Have A Dream" speech

☆ President Kennedy is assassinated

President Trivia Games

Who Am I?
2001-2009
See page 92

Trivia: Who was the second president of the United States?
See page 10

President Kennedy went to West Berlin in 1963 and delivered a speech condemning the Soviet Union for building the Berlin Wall. The wall (a mass of concrete and barbed wire that separated Communist East Berlin from non-Communist West Berlin) was built to stop Germans caught in the Soviet-controlled areas from fleeing to the non-Communist world. Despite the president's visit, the wall stayed erected and divided some families for several decades to come. It wasn't until 1989 (following the collapse of the Soviet Union) that the gates in the wall were opened to allow Germans from both sides to reunite.

President Kennedy with wife, Jackie, in the limousine in Dallas, Texas, on Main Street, minutes before the assassination

Tragically, while he was in Dallas, Texas, campaigning to be re-elected, Kennedy was shot and killed by Lee Harvey Oswald. The nation mourned its loss.

President John F. Kennedy (center right, standing at microphones) delivering remarks at Free University of Berlin in West Berlin, West Germany (Federal Republic)

> *I believe in an America where religious intolerance will someday end — where all men and all churches are treated as equal — where every man has the same right to attend or not attend the church of his choice.*
>
> —John F. Kennedy[37]

Approximately 5,000 people escaped to West Berlin when the Berlin Wall was in use and nearly 200 were killed trying. Some escaped by digging tunnels under the wall, others drove through security check points under a hail of bullet fire, and a few flew hot air balloons and ultralights over the barrier.

Lyndon B. Johnson

1963–1969

Democrat

Born: August 27, 1908

Died: January 22, 1973

#36

1963–1964

☆ Lyndon B. Johnson becomes president

☆ The Beatles appear on the *Ed Sullivan Show*

☆ Martin Luther King Jr. receives the Nobel Peace Prize

Lyndon Baines Johnson in Navy uniform

Lyndon B. Johnson (often referred to as LBJ) was born in Texas in 1908. He graduated from college in 1930 and became a high school teacher. A short time later, he entered politics and married Claudia Taylor. Together, they had two children and worked to get LBJ elected to a U.S. House seat. He won that election and several more.

During World War II, LBJ joined the Army, reported to General Douglas MacArthur, and was nearly shot down over the Pacific Ocean. After the war, he became a U.S. senator and a leader within the Democratic Party. He then joined John F. Kennedy in making a run for the White House. The election was close, but they won, and LBJ became America's new vice president.

Lyndon B. Johnson taking the oath of office aboard *Air Force One* after the assassination of John F. Kennedy

President Kennedy and Vice President Johnson on the White House south lawn

Lyndon B. Johnson became president after President Kennedy was killed. He then won the election of 1964. In office, he saw passage of the Civil Rights Act of 1964 (which outlawed racial segregation in many areas), signed the Voting Rights Act (which outlawed voter discrimination), and declared a war on poverty. These were all viewed as favorable to most people; however, after his popularity dwindled as a result of U.S. involvement in the Vietnam War and tax hikes, he didn't seek the presidency in 1968.

1965–1966

- ☆ U.S. combat troops arrive in Vietnam
- ☆ Bill Russell becomes first African American head coach in NBA

1967–1968

- ☆ Opposition to the Vietnam War grows
- ☆ Martin Luther King Jr. is assassinated
- ☆ Robert F. Kennedy is assassinated

President Trivia Games

Who Am I?

1953–1961

See page 74

Trivia: Who was president when the 1929 Stock Market Crash occurred?

See page 68

Israeli tanks advancing on the Golan Heights during the Six-Day War

The Six-Day War in June of 1967 between Israel (backed by the U.S.) and its neighbors of Egypt, Jordan, and Syria (backed by Russia) nearly led to armed conflict between the U.S. and Russia. Both powers had a naval presence in the eastern Mediterranean and tensions were high, but the U.S. and Russia showed restraint by allowing the warring nations to fight it out for themselves.

The year 1968 marked a dark period in American history. On April 4, civil rights leader Martin Luther King Jr. (he was also a Baptist minister) was shot while standing on a hotel balcony and died in surgery afterward. Two months later, civil rights activist and presidential hopeful Robert F. Kennedy (the younger brother of President John F. Kennedy) was shot after giving a speech. Kennedy died the following day as a result of his wounds.

Both King and Kennedy openly spoke about racial issues that were dividing the country, and many believe their deaths were the result of their calls for racial harmony.

> *I am not a theologian. I am not a philosopher. I am just a public servant that is doing the very best I know how. But in more than 3 decades of public life, I have seen first-hand how basic spiritual beliefs and deeds can shatter barriers of politics and bigotry.*
>
> —Lyndon B. Johnson[38]

Richard M. Nixon

1969–1974

#37

Republican

Born: January 9, 1913

Died: April 22, 1994

1969

- ☆ Richard M. Nixon takes office
- ☆ Neil Armstrong becomes the first man to walk on the moon
- ☆ *Mariner 7* makes fly-by of Mars

Election flyer/poster distributed on behalf of Richard Nixon's campaign for Congress, 1946

Richard Nixon sworn in as the 37th president by chief justice Earl Warren on January 20, 1969

Richard M. Nixon was born in 1913 in California. After obtaining degrees from both Whittier College and Duke University, he became a lawyer. He married Thelma Ryan in 1938 and, when World War II started, joined the U.S. Navy where he obtained the rank of lieutenant commander.

After the war, Nixon returned to California and began his political career. He served as both a U.S. representative and senator for California, and then became Dwight D. Eisenhower's vice president for two terms. As vice president, Nixon undertook many foreign trips of goodwill to promote U.S. Cold War policies. In 1960, he took a big step and ran for president; however, he lost this contest to John F. Kennedy.

Nixon giving his trademark "victory" sign during his successful campaign to become President of the United States

1970–1972

- ☆ First commercial flight of a Boeing 747 takes place

- ☆ China gets a seat on the United Nations Security Council
- ☆ U.S. swimmer Mark Spitz wins seven Olympic gold medals

1973

- ☆ Gerald R. Ford becomes VP after Spiro Agnew resigns

- ☆ Israel defeats Arab coalition in the Yom Kippur War

President Trivia Games

Who Am I?
1869–1877
See page 42

Trivia: Who was president during the Iran Hostage Crisis?
See page 84

After Nixon sat out of the 1964 election, he came back and won the 1968 and 1972 presidential elections. In the election of 1972, President Nixon defeated challenger George McGovern soundly. Nixon got 520 electoral votes to McGovern's 17. In office, he reduced American troop levels in Vietnam, airlifted weapons to Israel after it was attacked by Egypt and Syria, and was the first president to visit China.

Nixon family portrait with Julie and David Eisenhower, President Richard Nixon, First Lady Pat Nixon, Tricia and Edward Cox, 1971

Shortly after Israel's victory, it came to light that President Nixon was involved in a cover-up of illegal activities known as Watergate. Several men tied to President Nixon's administration were caught breaking into the Watergate complex trying to "tap" the phones of the Democratic National Committee. Later, President Nixon was caught in a series of lies trying to cover up his knowledge of the incident. So, rather than remaining president and possibly fighting the charges that were mounting against him, President Nixon resigned from office. He was the only U.S. president ever to resign.

A demonstrator demanding Nixon's impeachment

> *To me, the greatness of the universe is too much for man to explain. I still believe that God is the creator, the first cause of all that exists. I still believe that He lives today.*
>
> —Richard M. Nixon[39]

Gerald R. Ford

1974–1977

Republican

#38

Born: July 14, 1913

Died: December 26, 2006

1974

- ☆ President Nixon resigns
- ☆ Gerald R. Ford takes office
- ☆ President Ford pardons Nixon of all crimes

Gerald Ford on the football field at the University of Michigan, 1933

Gerald R. Ford was born in Nebraska in 1913. His birth name (which was changed following his mother's divorce and remarriage) was Leslie Lynch King Jr. Ford became a star athlete, helping his University of Michigan football team win national titles in 1932 and 1933, and later took a coaching job at Yale. A few years later, he was admitted to Yale Law School.

After graduating from law school, Ford returned to Michigan and opened a law practice in 1941. However, after Japan's attack on Pearl Harbor, he joined the naval reserves and fought in the Pacific.

The Gunnery officers of USS *Monterey*. Ford is second from the right, in the front row.

After the war, he married Elizabeth Warren and began a political career that took him to the U.S. House of Representatives. He later replaced Vice President Spiro Agnew, who resigned from office.

The Fords on their wedding day

Gerald R. Ford became president after President Nixon resigned in 1974. On September 8, 1974, President Ford granted President Nixon a full pardon for any crimes that he might have committed while in office. President Ford's decision upset many who thought that Nixon should have been put on trial for the Watergate Scandal mess. If you didn't know that a president could pardon someone of crimes, you do now!

1975

- ☆ Lynette Fromme attempts to assassinate President Ford
- ☆ Frank Robinson becomes MLB's first African American manager
- ☆ The Vietnam War comes to an end

1976

- ☆ Barbara Walters becomes America's first female nightly news anchor
- ☆ The U.S. Supreme Court upholds the death penalty

President Trivia Games

Who Am I?
1829–1837
See page 20

Trivia: Liberia named its capital in honor of this president.
See page 16

Jimmy Carter and Ford in a presidential debate

When the presidential election of 1976 came about, President Ford was able to win the Republican Party's nomination, but he was unable to win the big one. When his term ended, President Ford retired from politics. Did you know that President Ford is the only president not to be elected as either president or vice president? As Speaker of the House of Representatives, he became vice president when Spiro Agnew resigned and, later, president when Richard Nixon resigned.

The Vietnam War came to an end when the South Vietnamese capital of Saigon was overrun by North Vietnamese forces in 1975. While troops from the North were moving in, the U.S. evacuated more than 7,000 American citizens and "at-risk" Vietnamese by helicopter. North and South Vietnam became one nation under Communist rule shortly after America's withdrawal. So nearly nine months into his presidency, North Vietnam conquered South Vietnam, and U.S. involvement in the conflict essentially ended.

A marine getting his wounds treated during the Vietnam War

> "*As President, I have been cautioned to be very careful about what I say about religious matters. But the separation of church and state, although a fundamental principle to which I fully subscribe, was never intended, in my view, to separate public morality from public policy. It says that the power of government shall not be used to support or suppress any one faith, but in the same sentence protects the profession and the propagation of all faiths.*"
>
> —Gerald R. Ford[40]

James E. Carter

#39

1977–1981

Democrat

Born: October 1, 1924

Still living

1977

- ☆ Jimmy Carter takes office
- ☆ President Carter pardons almost all Vietnam draft evaders
- ☆ Atari 2600 becomes first successful home video gaming system

James Earl "Jimmy" Carter was born in 1924 in Georgia. He was a gifted student, excelled in basketball, and graduated from the U.S. Naval Academy in 1947. After serving six years in the navy, he returned to Georgia with his wife, Rosalynn, and took over his family's farm business. By 1970, he was considered a wealthy peanut farmer.

Campaign flyer from Democratic Party presidential primary, 1976

Carter's political career started in the Georgia Senate when racial segregation was the norm. In 1970, he ran for governor and refused to join the White Citizen's Council, a group favoring segregation. This angered many whites in Georgia but didn't stop Carter from winning the election. In office, he appointed many African Americans to state offices. He later won the Democratic Party's nomination for president in 1976.

President Carter with King Hussein of Jordan and the Shah of Iran

Jimmy Carter went on to win the presidential election of 1976. While in office, he worked to bring peace to various parts of the world; however, at home, an economic recession, high inflation, and an energy crisis hurt his popularity. Also, near the end of his term, 52 Americans were taken hostage in Iran for over a year, and the U.S. Olympic team was ordered to boycott the 1980 Summer Olympics. These problems contributed to his landslide defeat in the 1980 presidential election.

Jimmy Carter had the honor of having a Seawolf-class submarine named after him. The USS *Jimmy Carter* is one of a few ships in the U.S. Navy to have been named for a person who was alive at the time of the ship's naming.

The Iranian Hostage Crisis lasted from November 4, 1979, to January 20, 1981. It started when a group of militants and Islamist students stormed the U.S. Embassy in Iran and took American citizens hostage. During the 444-day crisis, negotiations to release the hostages took a turn for the worse when the U.S. military made a failed attempt to rescue the hostages. Operation "Eagle

1978–1979

- ☆ Margaret Brewer becomes U.S. Marine's first female general
- ☆ President Carter restores citizenship of Jefferson Davis
- ☆ Over 50 Americans are taken hostage in Iran

1980–1981

- ☆ The U.S. Olympic hockey team defeats Russia
- ☆ The U.S. Census counts 226 million Americans

- ☆ The American hostages in Iran are released

President Trivia Games

Who Am I?
1969–1974
See page 80

Trivia: Which president was Ronald Reagan's vice president?
See page 88

USS *Jimmy Carter* during the submarine's commissioning ceremony, February 19, 2005

Claw" (as it was called) resulted in the deaths of eight American soldiers and the loss of a C-130 Hercules and a few helicopters. However, despite the failed rescue attempt, the U.S. was able to broker a deal with Iran to free the hostages. The 52 Americans were formally released on January 20, 1981, just 20 minutes after Ronald Reagan was sworn into office.

The "Miracle on Ice" occurred during the 1980 Winter Olympics Games in New York when the U.S. hockey team (which consisted of college hockey players) defeated the mighty Soviet Union hockey team by a score of 4–3. Prior to the U.S. victory, the Soviets destroyed nearly everyone they faced, including a 6–0 route of the National Hockey League All-Star Team in an exhibition game!

Iranian students crowding the U.S. Embassy in Tehran, 1979

> *I've never let my beliefs interfere in my administration of the duties as President. But I've never found any incompatibility. I pray more than I did when I was not President, because the burdens on my shoulders are much greater than they were when I was a Governor or when I didn't hold public office.*
>
> —James E. Carter[41]

Ronald Reagan

#40

1981–1989

Republican

Born: February 6, 1911

Died: June 5, 2004

1981–1982

- ☆ Ronald Reagan takes office
- ☆ President Reagan is shot and wounded in failed assassination attempt
- ☆ Control of the Panama Canal is transferred to Panama

Ronald Wilson Reagan was born in 1911 in an Illinois apartment. He worked as a lifeguard, played sports, and was interested in acting. After a short stint as a radio sportscaster, he landed a contract with Warner Brothers studio and began a career in acting. Reagan later joined the military during World War II but could not serve overseas due to poor eyesight.

Ronald and Nancy Reagan waving during the Inaugural Parade in Washington, D.C., 1981

Ronald Reagan hosting *General Electric Theater*, 1960

Ronald Reagan won the presidential elections of 1980 and 1984 in electoral vote landslides. In office, he worked to improve America's economy and declining status as a superpower. He survived an assassination attempt, revamped the military, and escalated the Cold War with the Soviet Union.

In the end, his "peace through strength" philosophy helped lead to the collapse of the Soviet Union. In 1987, President Reagan went to the Berlin Wall in Germany and challenged Soviet leader Mikhail Gorbachev to "tear down this wall." After his second term ended, he retired from politics and returned to his ranch in California.

After the war, Reagan returned to the film industry and married Nancy Davis. He then turned his attention to politics and ran for governor of California. He won the election and served two terms before testing the waters for the presidency. In 1976, he challenged President Ford for the Republican Party's nomination and lost. Despite this setback, Reagan won more supporters and made a run to be the Republican Party's nominee four years later. This time around, he was successful.

The Reagans and William Frick standing behind the model of the aircraft carrier USS *Ronald Reagan*, 1996

1983–1984

- ☆ United States invades Grenada
- ☆ A national holiday is established to honor Martin Luther King Jr.

1985–1988

- ☆ 248 U.S. soldiers die in airplane crash in Newfoundland
- ☆ Seven U.S. astronauts die in Space Shuttle *Challenger* disaster
- ☆ Nearly 2,000 pro-life protestors are arrested

President Trivia Games

Who Am I?

1901–1909

See page 58

Trivia: Who was president during World War I?

See page 62

Reagan challenging Gorbachev to "tear down this wall"

Reagan helped bring economic growth to America. In comparison to the decade before, American homes of the 1980s saw technological advancements in many areas. Computers, home video games, microwave ovens, VCRs, cable television, and cell phones became commonplace in many homes.

Although President Reagan and Pope John Paul II avoided being assassinated in the 1980s, Egyptian President Anwar Sadat, former Beatles star John Lennon, and Indian Prime Minister Indira Gandhi did not. All three were shot to death.

Retro video recorder

> *Prayer has sustained our people in crisis, strengthened us in times of challenge, and guided us through our daily lives since the first settlers came to this continent. Our forbearers came not for gold, but mainly in search of God and the freedom to worship in their own way.*
>
> —Ronald Reagan[42]

George H.W. Bush

1989–1993

#41

Republican

Born: June 12, 1924

Died: November 30, 2018

1989–1990

- ☆ George H.W. Bush takes office
- ☆ A major earthquake in California delays baseball's World Series
- ☆ Douglas Wilder becomes first African American to be elected governor

George Herbert Walker Bush was born in Massachusetts in 1924. After the Japanese attack on Pearl Harbor, he postponed going to college and joined the U.S. Navy. He became the navy's youngest aviator at that time. After the war, he married Barbara Pierce, graduated from Yale University, and entered the oil business in Texas, later becoming a millionaire.

Chief Justice William Rehnquist administering the presidential oath of office to George H. W. Bush

Bush in his Grumman TBM Avenger aboard USS *San Jacinto*, 1944

After President Reagan served two terms, Bush ran for the presidency in 1988 and won. During his term, Iran invaded its neighbor, Kuwait. America and a coalition of allies then went to war to help small Kuwait and protect the world's oil supply. Iraq was easily defeated, but President Bush's popularity at home suffered when he broke a "no new tax" promise that he had made during his 1988 campaign for the White House. In siding with the Democratic Party and raising taxes, he angered many Republicans and was defeated by Bill Clinton, a Democrat, in the 1992 election.

By the age of 40, Bush was ready to enter politics. He won a seat to the U.S. House of Representatives in 1966 and later became the U.S. ambassador to the United Nations. He then changed roles by becoming the director of the CIA and, in 1981, Ronald Reagan's vice president. The old navy pilot was certainly flying high!

George H.W. Bush and Mikhail Gorbachev at the Helsinki Summit in 1990

1991

- ☆ The U.S. and its allies attack Iraq for occupying Kuwait

- ☆ The U.S. and its allies force Iraq to withdraw from Kuwait

1992

- ☆ VP Dan Quayle gets flak for spelling potato as "potatoe"
- ☆ Four policemen indicted in the Rodney King beating case

President Trivia Games

Who Am I?
1977–1981

See page 84

Trivia: Who became president after Abraham Lincoln was assassinated?

See page 40

President Bush meeting with General Colin Powell, Vice President Quayle, Secretary Dick Cheney, and others about the situation in the Persian Gulf and Operation Desert Shield, 1991

The American-led coalition consisted of nearly 1,000,000 troops, 2,000 aircraft, and 3,000 tanks. In comparison, Iraq had 500,000 troops, 700 aircraft, and 4,500 tanks. After the fighting started, Iraqi forces were overwhelmed by superior weaponry and suffered more than 30,000 casualties. When compared to the less than 500 coalition casualties, this war was one of the most lopsided in history.

Douglas Wilder made history on November 8, 1989, by becoming the first African American to be elected governor of a state. He defeated his challenger by less than half of a percent in the Virginia race and was sworn into office on January 13, 1990. In office, Governor Wilder focused on crime and gun control initiatives. He also ordered Virginia state agencies and universities to divest themselves of any investments in South Africa because of that nation's racist policy of apartheid. Because of Virginia's laws prohibiting successive gubernatorial terms, Wilder was unable to run for re-election in 1993.

A Kuwaiti M-84 main battle tank crossing a trench during a capabilities demonstration at a Kuwaiti outpost during Operation Desert Shield

Soon after Iraq invaded the small country of Kuwait in 1990, the United States joined a coalition of 34 nations and went to war against Iraq. The war (commonly referred to as the Gulf War, Operation Desert Storm, and the First Gulf War) ended in early 1991 after the coalition forces forced Iraq from Kuwait, destroyed much of Iraq's infrastructure and military forces, and imposed sanctions against Iraq.

> *I am guided by certain traditions. One is that there is a God and He is good, and his love, while free, has a self imposed cost: We must be good to one another.*
>
> —George H.W. Bush[43]

William J. Clinton

1993–2001

Democrat

Born: August 19, 1946

Still living

#42

1993–1995

☆ Bill Clinton takes office

☆ A Cessna airplane crashes on the White House lawn

☆ Oklahoma City bombing kills 168 people at a federal building

Governor and Mrs. Clinton attending the dinner honoring the nation's governors in the White House with President Ronald Reagan and first lady Nancy Reagan, 1987

William Jefferson "Bill" Clinton was born in Arkansas in 1946. As a student, he had many interests. He was an avid reader, a musician, and a student leader. While he was a member of Boys Nation, he got to visit the White House and meet President John F. Kennedy. This encounter was a huge influence on young Clinton.

Clinton graduated from Yale Law School in 1973 and married Hillary Rodham two years later. He returned to Arkansas where he became the state's attorney general and later its governor! Clinton held this position for nearly 12 years and helped Arkansas improve its economy and educational system. In 1992, he ran for president as the Democratic Party's nominee.

Bill Clinton taking the oath of office of President of the United States

Bill Clinton won the presidential elections of 1992 and 1996. In office, he signed the Family and Medical Leave Act of 1993, started the first official White House website, and helped fix a poor economy. In his second term, he was impeached based on allegations that he lied in a sworn deposition (i.e., perjury). He was found not guilty, though, and served out his final term. When he left office, President Clinton was still popular and had a job approval rating of more than 70 percent.

President Bill Clinton playing the saxophone presented to him by Russian President Boris Yeltsin

In 1999, the United States and other members of NATO launched a military operation against the military forces of the Federal Republic of Yugoslavia. During this era, Yugoslavia was divided among several different ethnic groups, its government and military were supporting the ethnic cleansing of several minority groups, and a civil war was raging. To prevent further acts against humanity, President Clinton committed

1996–1997

☆ One killed and many injured in bombing at the Atlanta Olympic Park

1998–2000

☆ Astronaut John Glenn, at the age of 77, returns to space

☆ U.S. Senate acquits President Clinton of lying under oath

☆ The U.S. Census counts 281 million Americans

President Trivia Games

Who Am I?
1981–1989
See page 86

Trivia: Who was president when two atomic bombs were dropped on Japan?
See page 72

President Bill Clinton with Nelson Mandela

U.S. troops to force the Yugoslavian government to end its internal conflict. The strategy worked, and U.N. peacekeeping forces soon entered the unstable nation to halt the ethnic unrest.

President Clinton's popularity showed when he easily defeated Republican Bob Dole and Reform candidate Ross Perot in the 1996 presidential election. With the win, Clinton became the first Democrat since President Franklin D. Roosevelt to be elected more than once.

Senator Hillary Clinton speaking during the second night of the 2008 Democratic National Convention

After serving as America's First Lady for eight years, Hillary Rodham Clinton began a political career. She became a U.S. senator in 2001 and nearly became the Democratic Party's candidate for president in 2008. In 2009, she gave up her Senate seat and became the secretary of state in President Obama's Administration. Finally, in 2016, she was the Democratic presidential nominee.

Bill and Hillary Clinton in New York, 2014

> *Sometimes I think the environment in which we operate is entirely too secular. The fact that we have freedom of religion doesn't mean we need to try to have freedom from religion. It doesn't mean that those of us who have faith shouldn't frankly admit that we are animated by the faith, that we try to live by it, and that it does affect what we feel, what we think, and what we do.*
>
> —Bill Clinton[44]

George W. Bush

#43

2001–2009

Republican

Born: July 6, 1946

Still living

2001

- ☆ George W. Bush takes office
- ☆ Terrorists launch 9/11 attacks on the U.S.
- ☆ The U.S. and its allies go to war in Afghanistan

George W. Bush in the Texas Air National Guard, where he served from 1968 to 1973

President Bush walking up the South Lawn toward the Oval Office with his son, George W. Bush

George Walker Bush, the son of President George H.W. Bush, was born in Connecticut in 1946. After graduating from Yale University with a degree in history, he earned a master's degree at Harvard Business School, married Laura Welch, and returned to Texas, his childhood home. Here, he entered politics and the oil business.

George W. and Laura Bush with their daughters Jenna and Barbara, 1990

After helping his father win the presidential election of 1988, George W. Bush bought a share in the Texas Rangers baseball franchise and then decided to run for governor of Texas. He won the election (focusing on court reform, crime reduction, and education) and took office in 1995. He was re-elected to a second term in 1998 and turned his sights to the White House. In 2000, he became the Republican Party's nominee for president.

George W. Bush became president after winning the elections of 2000 and 2004. In office, he was faced with the worst terror acts ever on U.S. soil (the 9/11 attacks on New York's Twin Towers and the Pentagon). Following the September 11, 2001,

2003–2005

- ☆ The U.S. and its allies go to war in Iraq
- ☆ A tsunami kills more than 260,000 people in Asia and Africa
- ☆ Hurricane Katrina slams New Orleans and the Gulf Coast

2007–2008

- ☆ Nancy Pelosi becomes America's first female Speaker of the House
- ☆ U.S. swimmer Michael Phelps wins eight Olympic gold medals

President Trivia Games

Who Am I?
1933–1945
See page 70

Trivia: Who was president during the War of 1812?
See page 14

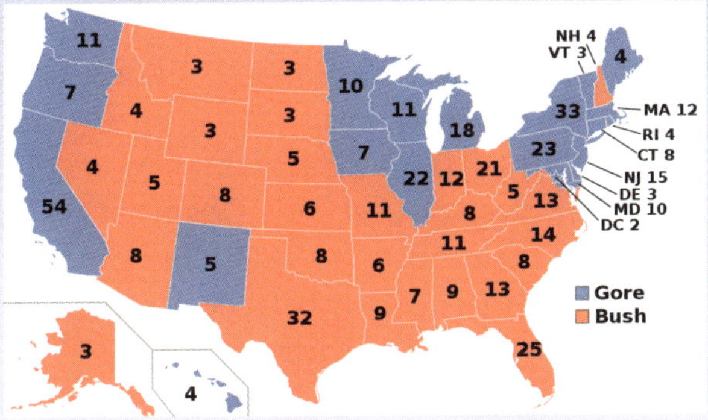

Results of the 2000 U.S. presidential election

terrorist attacks and the American-led invasion of Afghanistan, the U.S. and its allies went to war in Iraq under the name "Operation Iraqi Freedom." Suffering less than 200 casualties, America and its allies conquered Iraq swiftly and decisively. Iraq lost nearly 20,000 soldiers in the conflict. Following its defeat, Iraq was allowed to form a new government. Saddam Hussein, the former leader of Iraq, was executed by Iraq's new government for crimes against humanity.

Many Americans eventually wearied of the military's presence in these lands and President Bush's popularity declined. Then, after the Gulf of Mexico was hit by Hurricane Katrina, his popularity plummeted. After leaving office, President Bush retired from politics.

The north face of Two World Trade Center (south tower) immediately after being struck by United Airlines Flight 175

> *I pray on a daily basis. I've got a structure to my life where religion plays a role. I understand religion is a walk, it's a journey. And I fully recognize that I'm a sinner, just like you. That's why Christ died. He died for my sins and your sins.*
>
> —George W. Bush[45]

Barack Obama

2009–2017

Democrat

Born: August 4, 1961

Still living

#44

2009

- ☆ Barack Obama takes office
- ☆ The unemployment rate climbs above 10 percent

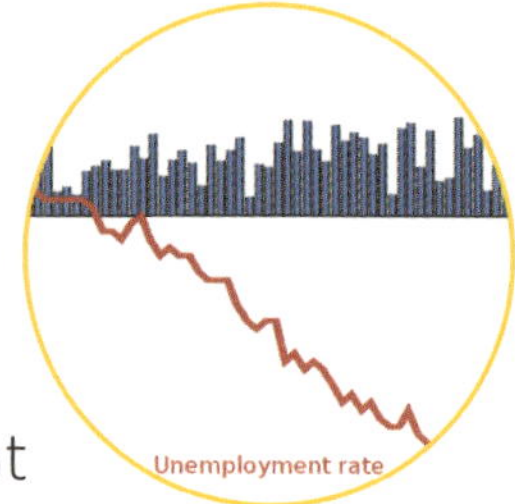

- ☆ The U.S. sends more troops to Afghanistan
- ☆ Over 700 grassroots "Tea Party" protests occur in one month

Obama family portrait in the Green Room of the White House, 2009

In 1985, Obama began work as a director of a church-based community organization that set up a job training program, tutoring program, and tenants' right organization. Three years later, he entered Harvard Law School where he obtained a law degree. Afterward, Obama began his political career by being elected to the Illinois state senate. A few years later, in 2004, he became one of that state's U.S. senators.

Barack Obama was born in Hawaii in 1961. In 1967, he moved with his family to Indonesia for four years. After returning to Hawaii, he attended a college "prep" school and graduated. He then went to Occidental College in Los Angeles before transferring to Columbia University where he obtained a B.A. in political science.

Barack Obama being sworn in as the 44th president of the United States by Chief Justice of the United States John G. Roberts, Jr.

President George W. Bush and President-elect Barack Obama meeting in the Oval Office of the White House.

Barack Obama won the presidential election of 2008, thus becoming the first African American to win the presidency, taking the oath of office on January 20, 2009. In his first few days in office, he signed a bill that provided insurance coverage to four million children that were uninsured. He also enacted economic stimulus packages to help improve America's poor economy and worked on reforming American health care. The cost of such programs has led to the national debt ballooning and the emergence of the "Tea Party," a voter movement looking for a fiscally sound, smaller federal government.

2010–2011

- ☆ BP oil rig disaster
- ☆ Osama bin Laden, the world's most wanted man, is killed by U.S. special forces

2014–2015

- ☆ "Black lives matter" protestors clash with police over death of Michael Brown
- ☆ Paris Climate Change Agreement

President Trivia Games

Who Am I?

1861–1865

See page 38

Trivia: Which president was a hero of the Spanish-American War?

See page 58

Barack Obama's "hope" and "change" message proved successful for many Democrats at the polls. Not only did Obama defeat Republican presidential nominee Senator John McCain easily, but Democrats running for Congress also benefited. After the votes were counted, the Democratic Party saw its 236–199 lead in the House of Representatives increase to 257–178 and its slim 51–49 Senate lead balloon to 59–41. For the first time in decades, Democrats had control of the White House and both houses of Congress!

Oh, how things can change. Exactly two years after gaining many congressional seats, the Democratic Party suffered major setbacks. When the votes were counted for the 2010 congressional elections, the Republican Party (with the help of the Tea Party movement) gained six seats in the Senate (cutting the Democratic advantage to 53–47) and even took control of the House. Still, despite these setbacks, Obama was easily re-elected president during the 2012 campaign.

During the second term of President Obama, the divisions between American ideologies came to the forefront — those bent toward socialism (a growing number of Democratic voters) and those bent toward a free-market society (mostly Republican voters) were more bitterly pitted against one another than any time before.

Since Obama couldn't serve another term (it's the law), his replacement within the Democratic Party was chosen to be Hillary Clinton — the former first lady under President Clinton. For many months, polls showed her easily beating her Republican opponent, Donald Trump—a candidate that never served in the military nor held a political position. Expectations were for her to easily be the next U.S. president (and the first female to hold this position), but she fell short on election night, November 8, 2016. She received a majority of the popular vote, but she significantly fell short in the electoral count (227 for Clinton, 304 for Trump).

Hillary Clinton campaigning in Raleigh, North Carolina, 2016

> *It wasn't until after college, when I went to Chicago to work as a community organizer for a group of Christian churches, that I confronted my own spiritual dilemma… And in time, I came to realize that something was missing as well — that without a vessel for my beliefs, without a commitment to a particular community of faith, at some level I would always remain apart, and alone.*
>
> —Barack Obama[46]

Donald Trump

2017–2021

Republican

Born: June 14, 1946

Still living

#45

2017

☆ Donald Trump takes office

☆ SpaceX conducts the world's first reflight of an orbital class rocket

☆ A total solar eclipse is visible within a band across the United States

Candidate Trump and running mate Mike Pence at the Republican National Convention, 2016

Donald Trump did what no other president before him had done. All his predecessors had either military or political experience to help them ascend to the highest position in the land, but Trump had none of these. Born and raised in New York, Trump inherited his father's rich estate and thereafter grew this wealth. He became a successful businessman, a fiery television personality, and a man of controversy. Feeling the need to do something more with his life, he tossed his hat into the political ring as a Republican in 2016 and defeated over ten other politically seasoned Republicans vying to become the party's nominee. A few months later, he shockingly won the presidential election over Democrat Hillary Clinton despite Clinton being a heavy favorite according to most professional political observers.

Trump's victory was stunning to the Democratic Party, the news media, and most within his party. At this pivotal historical moment, Americans were divided — nearly half leaned toward a socialist mindset (mainly those considering themselves members of the Democratic Party), and the other half leaned to a capitalistic mindset (mainly those from the Republican Party).

Trump's unexpected victory was so disturbing to those of the Democratic Party that it kicked off what was to become a four-year combat between two socio-economic philosophies. He was accused of working with foreign nations (primarily Russia) to win the 2016 election, and he was accused of being racist.

Nearly half of Americans supported Trump through his term — a term that showed many triumphs during its first three years despite the many legal challenges to his policies, opposition to his choices for federal judges to be appointed, his pro-life support, his war with the media, and endless investigations against him.

Trump recognized Jerusalem as Israel's capital (something no other nation was willing to do) and helped to broker peace deals between Israel, Morocco, Sudan, United Arab Emirates, and Bahrain, known as the "Abraham Accords."

First meeting of the Cabinet of Donald Trump in the White House

2018

- ☆ Trump meets with North Korean leader Kim Jong-un

- ☆ *Washington Post* journalist Jamal Khashoggi is murdered inside the Saudi consulate in Istanbul, Turkey

2019–2021

- ☆ Trump impeached (2019)
- ☆ The World Health Organization declares the COVID-19 outbreak a pandemic

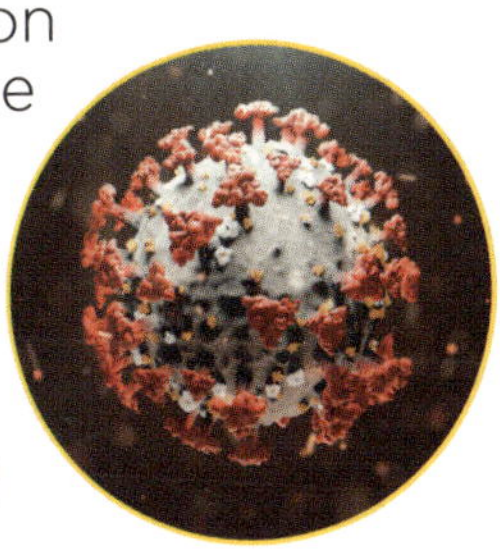

- ☆ Trump impeached a second time (2021)

President Trivia Games

Who Am I?
1909–1913
See page 60

Trivia: Who was the first president of the United States?"
See page 8

Trump signs the Coronavirus Preparedness and Response Supplemental Appropriations Act

He instituted policies that led to unseen advances in the U.S. economy and focused on protecting American works and industries. The U.S. became the world's leading producer of crude oil in 2018, the poverty rate for African Americans and Hispanic Americans reached their lowest levels since the U.S. began collecting such data, and the economy added over seven million more jobs than in Obama's last year in office.

However, something unexpected happened. A once-in-a-lifetime virus struck the world near the beginning of Trump's final year in office. The coronavirus — which originated in China — hit every nation on the earth, starting in 2019, and caused great upheaval. The media ran stories for many months declaring Trump at fault for the pandemic reaching and spreading across American soil, coupled with increased claims of racial discrimination, police brutality, and other social injustices.

When it came time for the 2020 presidential election, nearly half of the U.S. population didn't like Trump and much of the media was bent on seeing his defeat. As for leaders within his own Republican Party, most of them were hesitant in their support, and this aided in his failing re-election bid.

The coronavirus hit like a storm. Compared to the 1919 Spanish Flu, total deaths and the death rate from COVID-19 were slightly lower in comparison. On top of that, Trump faced a propaganda war from his political opponents, the media, and even members from within his party. Unfortunately for him, he had to carry all this into the 2020 presidential election.

Trump lost his 2020 re-election attempt by a slim margin to his Democratic opponent. His administration produced many lawsuits declaring voting fraud, but these lawsuits fell short in the judiciary branch (the courts) and he was defeated.

> *Our rights are not given to us by man; our rights come from our Creator. No matter what, no Earthly force can take those rights away. That is why the words "Praise be to God" are etched atop the Washington Monument, and those same words are etched into the hearts of our people.*
>
> —Donald Trump[47]

Joe Biden

2021–present

#46

Democrat

Born: November 20, 1942

Still living

2021

☆ Thousands of angry far right Republicans and some leftist Democrats storm the U.S. Capitol building

Biden and his second wife, Jill, met in 1975 and married in 1977.

Joseph "Joe" Biden was born and raised in Scranton, Pennsylvania, in 1942. At the age of 13, he moved with his family to Mayfield, Delaware, where he was often teased by school mates for a stuttering issue — an impediment he eventually overcame. He later attended the University of Delaware, where he played football and developed an interest in politics. While in school, he also met his future wife (Neilia Hunter). Biden and Hunter married in 1966 while he was attending the Syracuse University Law School.

Upon graduation, Biden moved to Wilmington, Delaware, to practice law and enter politics. His political career began with his being elected councilman in Delaware's New Castle County in 1970. He was encouraged to run as a Democrat for the U.S. Senate, and with the odds stacked against him, Biden won the 1972 election and became one of the youngest U.S. senators ever elected.

Sadly, tragedy struck before Biden took office. He, his wife, and three children were involved in a car accident shortly before Christmas. Neilia and his daughter were both killed, and Biden's two sons were severely injured. Still, despite the emotional toll, Biden remained committed to serving his state and took his oath of office while standing next to the hospital bed of one of his sons.

Biden served as senator from 1973 to 2009, and during that time, he met and married Jill Jacobs. As senator, he became respected for his diligent work and stances on many issues. In 2008, Barack Obama, the Democrat nominee for president, selected him to be his running mate for the 2008 presidential election.

Obama and Biden won the 2008 campaign. Thus Biden assumed the role of vice president of the United States. He held this post for eight years during President Obama's two terms. After the second term ended, Biden bowed out of politics for four years and came out of retirement to campaign as a presidential candidate for the 2020 election.

President Barack Obama presenting Vice President Joe Biden with the Presidential Medal of Freedom

2021

☆ Many American businesses on lockdown by executive orders from state governors due to the coronavirus outbreak

2021

☆ As of January, reports claim that over 2 million people have died worldwide due to COVID-19; the U.S. accounted for over 400,000 of these deaths

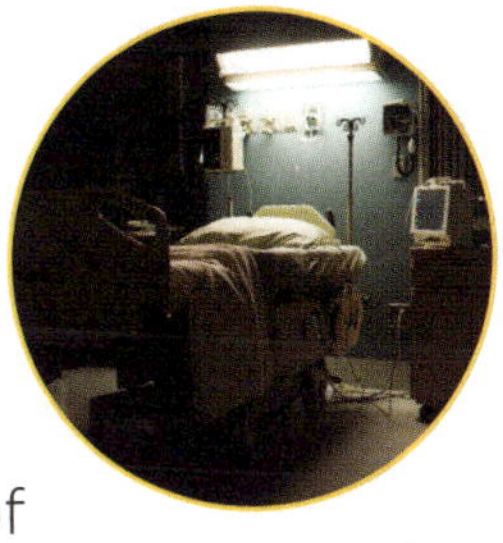

President Trivia Games

Who Am I?
1923–1929
See page 66

Trivia: Who was governor of Arkansas prior to becoming president?
See page 90

Biden became the nominee of the Democrat Party and went on to defeat President Donald Trump in the general election. The final electoral count showed Biden with 306 votes and Trump with 232 votes. Biden won the popular tally as well by receiving somewhere over 81 million votes to Trump's 74 million votes.

2017 image of United States Senator Kamala Harris

Kamala Harris was Joe Biden's choice for vice president. She became the first woman and the first non-white person to hold that office!

Joe Biden took the oath of office on January 20, 2021, thus becoming the oldest person ever elected to the presidency. As Joe Biden begins his four-year term, the country is divided, waiting to see what this president will do. Will he bring unity, or continue to polarize a divide nation? His first priorities will be reducing the impact of the coronavirus and helping build back the struggling U.S. economy. As Christians, there is always a need to lift our leaders in prayer and to trust God no matter who is placed in leadership over us.

Joe Biden taking the oath of office as president on the West Front of the U.S. Capitol Building on January 20, 2021

> *The Bible tells us that to everything there is a season — a time to build, a time to reap, a time to sow. And a time to heal. This is the time to heal in America.*
>
> —Joe Biden[48]

Glossary of Terms

Congress – The U.S. Senate and the U.S. House of Representatives make up Congress. Together, they create bills that may become laws.

Election Day – For the president and vice president, election day occurs on the Tuesday after the first Monday in November within years that are evenly divisible by four. On this day, voters go to the polls. After a state tallies its votes, it selects electors to the electoral college that will eventually meet with other state electors to formally vote for the president and vice president.

Electoral College – This is a body of elected representatives (called electors) who formally elect the president and vice president. The number of electors each state has is equal to its number of U.S. Senators and Representatives. Oh, and Washington, D.C., gets a few too!

Electoral Votes – Each elector in the electoral college gets to cast one vote for the president and another for the vice president. In most cases, a state's electors cast all their votes for the same candidate(s).

First Lady – This is the president's wife.

House of Representatives – This is one of the two Houses of the U.S. Congress. (The other House of Congress is called the Senate.) Its total number of representatives is currently limited to 435, and each representative serves a two-year term. Representatives are apportioned to each state based upon that state's population and elected by voters from within the states.

Impeachment – Impeachment is when formal charges are brought by members of legislature against a civil officer of government, including the president. If the charges are sufficient, a trial could take place and the individual could be removed from office.

Inauguration Day – This is the day that a newly elected president takes office. Before 1933, Inauguration Day was March 4. With the passage of the 20th Amendment, it has occurred on January 20.

Senate – This is one of the two Houses of the U.S. Congress. (The other is the House of Representatives.) Its total number is limited to two members (or senators) from each state (100). Each senator serves a six-year term and is elected by voters from the state.

Speaker of the House – The Speaker of the House is the presiding officer of the U.S. House of Representatives. This person is chosen by the House of Representatives and is second in the United States presidential line of succession, just behind the vice president.

President pro tempore – The president pro tempore is the highest-ranking senator in the U.S. Senate and presides over its sessions in the absence of the vice president (who is actually the president of the Senate). The president pro tempore is selected by members of the Senate and is third in the United States presidential line of succession, just behind the Speaker of the House of Representatives.

Supreme Court – The U.S. Supreme Court is composed of a Chief Justice and eight Associate Justices. These judges usually serve for life and hear many cases involving the law. They are the guardian and interpreter of the U.S. Constitution.

Political Party – Political parties are formed when people with similar goals unite to elect individuals who share their viewpoints. There have been many political parties in U.S. history. The Democratic Party and the Republican Party are the two largest ones today.

President – The president is the head of the executive branch of the U.S. Federal Government.

Veto – Veto is the Latin word for "I forbid." If the president doesn't want a bill to become law when it reaches his desk, he can veto it unless there is a two-thirds vote in the House and Senate to override it.

Vice President – The vice president is first in the United States presidential line of succession. He is also president of the U.S. Senate.

Endnotes

[1]From George Washington to the Hebrew congregation in Newport, Rhode Island, 1790

[2]Adams wrote this on June 28, 1813, excerpt from a letter to Thomas Jefferson

[3]Notes on the State of Virginia, Query XVIII, p. 237

[4]Letter to Frederick Beasley, Nov. 20, 1825

[5]To his daughter Eliza

[6]John Quincy Adams, An Oration Delivered Before the Inhabitants of the Town of Newburyport at Their Request on the Sixty-First Anniversary of the Declaration of Independence, July 4, 1837 (Newburyport: Charles Whipple, 1837), pp. 5-6

[7]Statement made during his final illness, June 1, 1845

[8]Martin Van Buren's Inaugural Address, March 4, 1837

[9]Inaugural Address, 4 March 1841

[10]First annual message to Congress, June 1, 1841

[11]Inaugural Address, March 4, 1845

[12]Hickey, William (1853). *The Constitution of the United States of America*. T. K. & P. G. Collins, Page 334.

[13]Letter to Henry Clay, November 11, 1844

[14]First Annual Message, December 5, 1853

[15]*Presidential Leadership: Rating the Best and the Worst in the White House* (2004) edited by James Taranto and Leonard Leo.

[16]The House Divided speech (1858)

[17]Written shortly before his death, July 1875

[18]Personal Memoirs of General U. S. Grant (1885)

[19]Diary, October 15, 1884

[20]Letter to Colonel A. F. Rockwell, August 13, 1866

[21]Veto message of Rivers and Harbor Bill (1882)

[22]Letter to Rev. Wilton Merle Smith, D.D., March 21, 1906

[23]Statement of 1888, as quoted in *Treasury of Presidential Quotations* (1964) by Caroline T. Hamsberger

[24]Letter of Acceptance as Candidate for Governor (Oct. 7, 1882)

[25]First Inaugural Address (March 4, 1897)

[26]Theodore Roosevelt's "Nine Reasons for Going to Church," 1917.

[27]https://www.brainyquote.com/quotes/mark_twain_717886.

[28]Address in Pocatello, Idaho (5 October 1911)

[29]Speech at New York Press Club (9 September 1912)

[30]Relayed by Bishop William F. Anderson as a remark by a friend of Harding, in "Pictures Harding as Man of Prayer" (2 April 1922) *New York Times*

[31]*New Day*, 1928

[32]https://obamawhitehouse.archives.gov/1600/presidents/herberthoover.

[33]Address to the Nebraska Republican Conference, Lincoln, Nebraska (January 16, 1936)

[34]Address to Congress after the attack on Pearl Harbor (December 8, 1941)

[35]Address at a Luncheon of the National Conference of Christians and Jews, November 11, 1949

[36]Flag Day speech, signing bill authorizing addition of the words "under God" to the Pledge of Allegiance, 14 June 1954

[37]Address to the Ministerial Association of Greater Houston, September 12, 1960

[38]Remarks to the Southern Baptist Christian Leadership Seminar, March 25, 1964

[39]"What Can I Believe?" (college essay), 9 October 1933 (quoted in RN: The Memoirs of Richard Nixon, 1978, p. 16)

[40]Remarks at the Annual Congressional Breakfast of the National Religious Broadcasters, January 28, 1975

[41]Question & answer session at a townhall meeting, Independence, Missouri, September 2, 1980

[42]Remarks at a White House Ceremony in Observance of National Day of Prayer, May 6, 1982

[43]Convention Acceptance, 1988

[44]Remarks at a White House Interfaith Breakfast, August 30, 1993

[45]"George W. Bush: Running on His Faith," *US News* Online

[46]Address, Sojourners/Call to Renewal "Building a Covenant for a New America" Conference, Washington, D.C., June 26, 2006

[47]Annual National Prayer Breakfast, February 8, 2018

[48]"Biden's faith comes through in speech, quoting Catholic hymn and Bible verse" by Courtney Subramanian, *USA TODAY* - published November 7, 2020

Create your own timeline of world history!

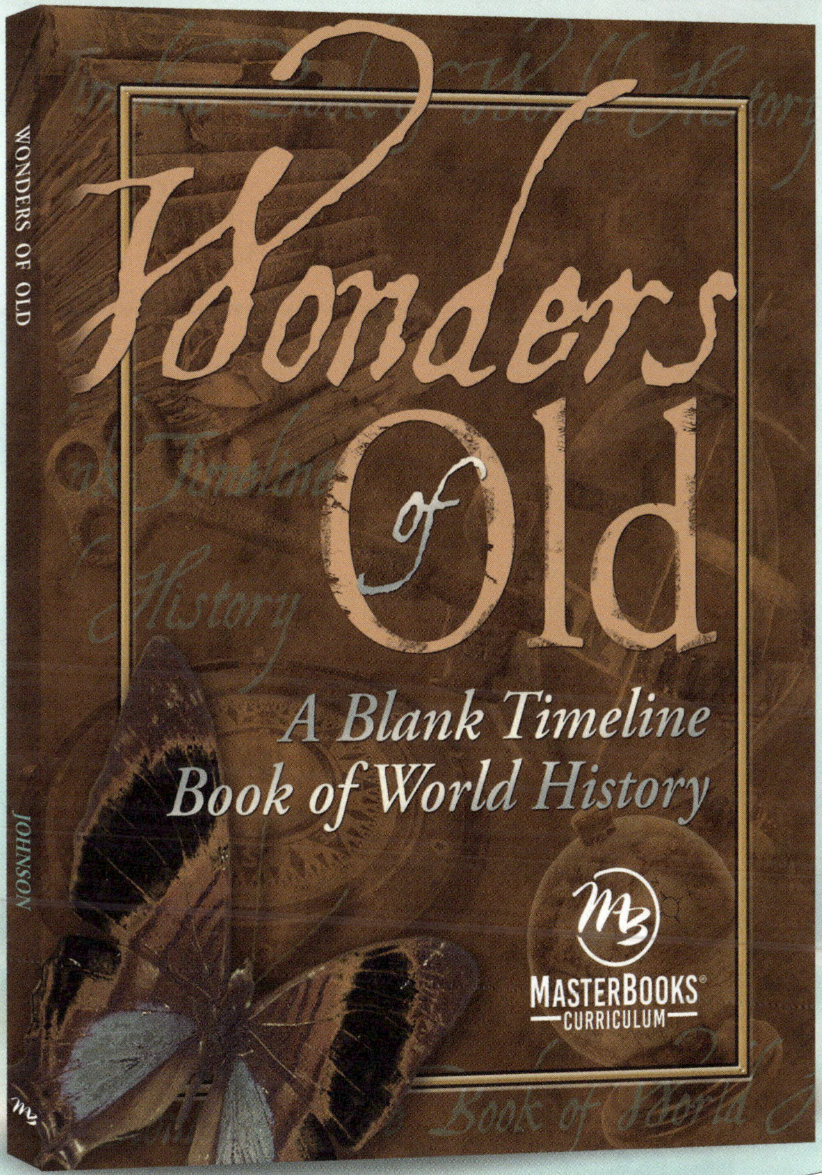

978-1-68344-272-1

This blank timeline book with dates pre-marked from BC to the present provides your student with a better understanding of the flow of history.

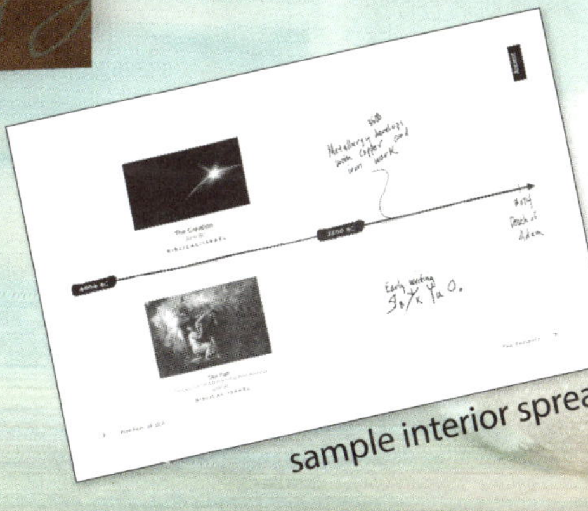

sample interior spread

MASTERBOOKS® CURRICULUM

AVAILABLE AT MASTERBOOKS.COM & OTHER PLACES WHERE FINE BOOKS ARE SOLD.

Language Lessons for a Living Education

GRADE 1
LANGUAGE LESSONS FOR A LIVING EDUCATION 1
978-1-68344-211-0

GRADE 2
LANGUAGE LESSONS FOR A LIVING EDUCATION 2
978-1-68344-122-9

GRADE 3
LANGUAGE LESSONS FOR A LIVING EDUCATION 3
978-1-68344-137-3

GRADE 4
LANGUAGE LESSONS FOR A LIVING EDUCATION 4
978-1-68344-138-0

GRADE 5
LANGUAGE LESSONS FOR A LIVING EDUCATION 5
978-1-68344-178-6

GRADE 6
LANGUAGE LESSONS FOR A LIVING EDUCATION 6
978-1-68344-209-7

VISIT **MASTERBOOKS.COM** *Where Faith Grows!* **TO SEE OUR FULL LINE OF FAITH-BUILDING CURRICULUM OR CALL 800-999-3777**